# It's a PC World

# It's a PC World

### How to Live in a World
### Gone Politically Correct

## Edward Stourton

HODDER &
STOUGHTON

First published in Great Britain in 2008 by Hodder & Stoughton
An Hachette Livre UK company

1

Copyright © Edward Stourton 2008

A CIP catalogue record for this title is available from the British Library

ISBN 978 0340 954867

Typeset in New Caledonia by Palimpsest Book Production Ltd,
Grangemouth, Stirlingshire

Printed and bound by Clays Ltd, St Ives plc

Hodder & Stoughton policy is to use papers that are natural, renewable and
recyclable products and made from wood grown in sustainable forests.
The logging and manufacturing processes are expected to conform
to the environmental regulations of the country of origin.

Hodder & Stoughton Ltd
338 Euston Road
London NW1 3BH

www.hodder.co.uk

*To Kudu the Springer Spaniel, faithful companion in my writer's shed and tireless enthusiast for ruminative walks.*

# Contents

# Acknowledgements

I owe thanks to almost everyone I have met during the year it took me to write this book for their contributions to my research; rare indeed are those who do not have strong views of some kind about its subject. Sometimes I followed up a casual conversation with a more detailed interview; the colleagues and friends who helped me in this way will find themselves mentioned in the text, and I owe them particular gratitude.

To those who have provided me with examples of numbskull abominations of the English language, sloppy thinking and preposterous propositions my thanks may be less welcome, but, truly, I could not have done this without you. To the wiser writers and thinkers, many of them long dead, who helped me keep an anchor in sanity, I say the same, with admiration.

My children Ivo, Eleanor and Tom and my step-daughter Rosy provided me with material by being themselves – and together with my wife Fiona acted as occasional editors. When they united in the opinion that

I had written something so foolish that it would embarrass them all, I removed it.

Judith Longman, my editor at Hodder, seems to have a better sense of what I should be writing than I do; this subject was her idea, and after a little *prima donna*-ish fussing I realised what a good one it was. Vivienne Schuster, my agent, read the first half of my manuscript and, at just the moment when my creative bio-rhythms were flagging, gave me the encouragement I needed to keep going. Both of them managed my occasional angst-attacks with exemplary patience.

# Introduction to a PC World

I spent a terrifyingly high proportion of my early broad-casting career preparing for the death of the Queen Mother; past counting were the Sundays given over to the curious ritual known as Royal Death Rehearsals.

We would all troop into the office pretending it was a day like any other, and then affect surprise when a wire purporting to be from the Press Association pinged us into life; there would be a report that one of the ghillies at the Castle of Mey had been spotted ringing 999 at the local post office, or a rumour that all leave had been cancelled for the choir at the Abbey. An elaborate scenario dreamt up by one of the bosses would then unfold in 'as live' conditions, and at some point one had to make the Big Decision about whether to put on The Black Tie. There was a cupboard in the newscasters' make-up room where we all kept an appropriately funereal outfit; the names on the suits went back through several generations of newscasters and correspondents and served as a slightly chilling reminder of professional mortality. These rehearsals were not occasions to be taken lightly, and

1

while the Queen Mother herself survived years of them one sometimes felt, at the programme post-mortem, that one's own career would not.

You may imagine, then, the thrill of receiving an invitation to lunch with this near-mythic creature who had ruined so many of my weekends. And not just any old lunch – this was to be an intimate affair at a private house in Windsor Great Park. It was the 1990s, and since the Queen Mother was, in the phrase I had heard countless times in her rehearsed obituaries, 'as old as the century', I could not help being impressed by the sprightly figure who bounced in and immediately started living up to her stereotypes, knocking back the gin and Dubonnet and twinkling away with rude enthusiasm. After lunch each of us was required to sit alone with her for a while. She inquired, with what seemed like very genuine interest, after my children, and I was impressed again; perhaps all those wasted Sundays were justified. Then she asked me what I had been doing recently – and, grateful for a topic that might keep us going for a while in a general way, I explained that I was just back from a European Union summit.

'It will never work, you know,' she declared. Bemused, I asked her what she thought would 'never work'. 'The EEC,' she said, using a term that was already long out of date, 'it will never work with all those Huns, Wops and Dagos.' The words were delivered with the eyes on maximum, tiara-strength twinkle, but I am afraid I froze.

The Nation's Favourite Grandmother was, I thought, in fact a ghastly old bigot, a prey to precisely the kind of prejudice which had driven the conflicts the European project had been designed to prevent. I suffered what I am sure some would say was a terrible sense of humour failure – I thought that what she had said was nasty and ugly. The phrase 'politically correct' was not much used in those days, but that is what I felt the Queen Mother most emphatically was not, and I was shocked. Fortunately, by the time she finally shuffled off this mortal coil I had left television news for *Today*, and I never had to run the risk that my views on her would compromise the grave-voiced, misty-eyed tone of a real Royal Death (Category One) programme.

A decade and a half later I was interviewing a retired but still extremely active – and thoughtful – senior military man on the *Today* programme. The idea of British troops withdrawing from southern Iraq had been floated that morning and I asked him whether he thought the Iraqi army and police were sufficiently well prepared to take full responsibility for security in and around Basra. The army, he told me, was coming on well, but he feared that the police would prove to be – and these quotation marks are most emphatic – 'the nigger in the woodpile'.

I completely believe the theory that a drowning man sees his whole life flash before his eyes before he goes, because at a live broadcasting moment like that the world really does slow down; my pause probably sounded like a nanosecond to the listeners, but to me it felt as if the memories of all the bad moments in a quarter of a century of broadcasting experience were flashing back and forth across my synapses as I desperately tried to formulate an appropriate response – if my fellow presenter had told me that my forehead was actually glowing I should not have been at all surprised. Should I pick the General up on that remark – thus demonstrating my sensitivity to the unfortunate implications of his turn of phrase, but at the same time probably throwing him into complete confusion and plunging us all into a ferment of embarrassment? Or should I simply ignore it, hoping that most of our listeners would conclude that it was a slip of the tongue and should not be allowed to detract from the thrust of his overall argument?

I took a deep breath and pretended that nothing had happened. I had often talked to the General in question over the *Today* programme breakfast trolley, and I did not think he was a racist; he had, I calculated, simply forgotten himself in the odd intimacy of a radio interview over the telephone and used an expression which – however offensive it may sound today – had once been relatively commonplace in certain circles, military ones undoubtedly included. When I burst out of the studio at the first available opportunity – a bit like a pearl-diver bursting to the surface for air after some ghastly encounter with a creature of the deep – a whey-faced editor tried to comfort me with some not very reassuring words:

'There is no right response to something like that,' he said.

Often – by no means always – one makes a better judgement on questions 'like that' in the heat of battle than one would do if the matter had been endlessly war-gamed in BBC committees; perhaps that is precisely because the warp-speed debate that goes on in your head forces you back on instinct. There were plenty of emails complaining that I should have picked him up for using the expression, but at the turn of the next hour on the programme we broadcast an apology from the General, who was by now feeling thoroughly embarrassed himself, and the matter was pretty much laid to rest. He still broadcasts on the BBC, and the importance of the point he was trying to make – that constructing an honest and non-partisan Iraqi police force was proving a real challenge – has been demonstrated all too clearly by subsequent events.

The Queen Mother's comments fundamentally changed my views about her – the General's slip did not change my views about him. This book is an attempt to navigate the waters that lie between the General and the Queen Mother.

And they are difficult waters to navigate. The phrase 'Political Correctness gone mad' is thrown about so often and so casually these days that it makes me, well, mad really, though in the sense of angry rather than barmy. It is often followed by a piece of sloppy journalism – a story which has been made to sound ludicrous by careful editing of the facts. A particularly enjoyable example in the *Daily Mail* caught my eye just as I was beginning work on this book. It concerned a plan for a 'multi-cultural reinterpretation' of the York Mystery Plays which was put forward by the city council as part of a bid for lottery money. 'Since the 14th century, actors and actresses have taken to the streets of York to depict the great moments in Biblical history, from the Creation to the last judgement of Christ,' declares the lead paragraph, 'But the Medieval Mystery Plays are threatened by a 21st century curse – of political correctness.'

Like most journalists, slap-dash tribe that we are, I resent time spent checking facts, and one of the reasons I so much enjoyed this piece was that there was no need for anything tiresome like phoning a press officer; the text very thoughtfully pointed out its own weaknesses. That ringing clarion call of an opening sentence was somewhat undermined by this, in the penultimate paragraph: 'religious upheaval during the 16th century led to the plays being stopped in 1569. They were revived in 1951 and have proved a popular crowd-puller ever since.' Hmmm. So we are not quite talking about six centuries of uninterrupted pageantry performed by generation upon generation of free-born Englishmen, then. It also turns out that for most of the period since the revival of the plays during the Festival of Britain, they have been performed on a fixed stage, so that 'taken to the streets

of York to depict the great moments in Biblical history'
is not quite right either.

And what was happening in 1569, when the plays were
banned? 'Religious upheaval' is a rather polite way to
describe a period of Catholic rebellion (the Rising of the
North took place in the autumn of that year) and brutal
anti-Catholic persecution. Some not very energetic investigation reveals that the York Mystery Plays were
suppressed by the Elizabethan authorities for being too
Catholic – even though scenes honouring the Virgin Mary
had been cut in an attempt to placate Protestant sensibilities. Since Protestantism was the 'politically correct'
religion of the day it is reasonable to say that the plays
were, in fact, victims of sixteenth-century Political
Correctness. And being un-PC in those days carried a
rather more serious risk than finding yourself the target
of a rude editorial in the *Guardian* – you might be locked
up in the Tower, say, and hanged, drawn and quartered
after a show trial, or you might be beheaded (which is
what happened to the leader of the Rising of the North,
the Earl of Northumberland) or even, if you were found
hiding a Catholic priest and refused to talk about it,
crushed to death (Margaret Clitherow, who, as a young
girl growing up as the sheriff's daughter in York, would
have seen the last of the original Mystery Plays, was, in
1586, 'laid out upon a sharp rock, and a door was put on
top of her and loaded with an immense weight of rocks
and stones. Death occurred within fifteen minutes'). None

of this quite fits the tone of the *Mail* 'line', as it suggests that the idea of ideological 'correctness' has a long pedigree in Britain, and is not simply a twenty-first-century 'curse' dreamt up by a group of ethnically diverse New Labour lesbian spin-doctors.

'Precisely how the age-old stories featuring Adam and Eve and Jesus Christ and his apostles will be "revitalised" for a multi-cultural society has yet to be revealed,' the *Mail* admits – so you might think it would be a bit difficult to get too worked up about it all. Not a bit of it. 'It has been admitted' – oh, horror of horrors – 'that *refugees and actors from foreign countries* could be asked to participate.' My italics, I confess. At this point I began to wonder whether the whole thing was some kind of subversive joke perpetrated by a Troskyite entryist who had inveigled his way on to the staff of the *Mail*. 'Traditionalists,' we were told, 'are outraged.' Really? Then why is there almost no 'outrage' in direct quotation? Real traditionalists would of course know that there has been a longstanding debate about whether medieval Mystery Plays in general are anti-Semitic, so the idea of multicultural revisionism in this context is not entirely new. Plus, of course, the Mystery Plays were originally a form of 'community theatre' performed by the city's artisan guilds, so it is perfectly tenable to argue that revisionism to reflect the nature of York's contemporary community is very much in keeping with 'tradition'.

And yet the mere fact that a successful mass-circulation paper like the *Mail* runs pieces of this kind tells us

8

something. Staff on the *Daily Telegraph* had a wonderful expression to describe those prurient stories the paper used to report on page 3 about naughty vicars and the like; they were called 'marmalade droppers', the idea being that the ghastly details would make Colonel Bufton-Tufton's hand shake uncontrollably with outrage and excitement as he navigated the journey between plate and mouth, causing a dollop of Oxford Thick Cut to be deposited on the breakfast table. 'Political Correctness gone mad' stories are today's marmalade droppers. They touch on what in American political jargon are known as 'hot button issues', the raw, visceral stuff of politics which can stir debate in a manner that managerial policy wonkery never can. PC – whatever it means exactly – is a phenomenon that makes many people in this country feel uncomfortable, and it will not do to dismiss them all as block-headed bigots.

The way our thinking and behaviour in this area has altered over the past few years represents something close to a genuine cultural revolution, and, like any big change, the birth of a PC World has come at a cost. When I began writing this book, my prejudice – in so far as I had one – was towards the belief that that cost was relatively modest: that we pay it only in our mild irritation at the loss of certain words or phrases, or in our sadness when stories we enjoyed as children are judged offensive by changing fashion. But as I have explored the geography of our PC World – it is, I now realise, vast, and I am sure some of you will feel I have left large parts of it uncharted – I have been forced to confront some really quite serious questions. Big Issues like identity, freedom of speech, honesty in political discourse, discrimination and religious tolerance lie like rocky outcrops just beneath the frothy waters of the teasing fun that is to be had at the expense of PC zealots. And despite the uncharitable comments I have made above about the *Daily Mail's* coverage of the York Mystery Plays saga, the PC challenge to our understanding of history is among the most serious of those issues – and I shall be returning to it in the last chapter of this book.

One of the very good jokes about Time in Laurence Sterne's novel *Tristram Shandy* revolves around the eponymous hero's addiction to digression; somewhere in Volume Four he reflects that it has taken a year to describe the first day of his life, and concludes that the more he writes, the further he will fall behind with his project of recording his *Life and Opinions*. The writing of this book was a bit like that; I so often had to revise what I had written in the light of a new marmalade dropper that the arrival of our daily paper delivery became a source of weary anxiety. The story I am trying to tell is changing all the time, and, like all the best stories, it is full of unexpected and shocking twists and turns. On the afternoon when Rowan Williams made his notorious comments about Sharia law I bicycled to the gym to clear my head after a hard day's writing; I was almost assaulted there by a complete stranger who apparently thought that it was reasonable to berate me about the iniquity of the Archbishop's comments – presumably on the basis that being a radio presenter made me, in the vaguest possible way, a public figure. Rage had reduced her to incoherence, but when she squeaked out the words 'Political Correctness gone mad' I could almost hear the great shout of support from the shires of middle England.

So my journey through a PC World really is a voyage of discovery. If you choose to accompany me I should say frankly at the outset that I shall set out to confuse you. This is such an important subject that muddle-headedness is the only possible way to respond to it.

# 1

# The origins of the PC species

I would say it [the PC debate] looks like the Battle of
Waterloo as described by Stendhal. A murky fog hangs
over the field. Now and then a line of soldiers marches
past. Who are they? Which army do they represent? They
may be Belgian deconstructionists from Yale, or perhaps
the followers of Lionel Trilling in exile from Columbia.
Perhaps they are French mercenaries. It is impossible to
tell. The fog thickens. Shots go off. The debate is unintel-
ligible. But it is noisy!

Paul Berman, *Debating PC: The Controversy over*
*Political Correctness on College Campuses*

A definition would be a sensible way to begin, were
it not for the fact that trying to define the term
'Political Correctness' is a little like trying to write a
neutral history of the Middle East – the way you tell it
depends very much on where you stand. If I was a paid-
up PC-er, I might argue that the phrase describes a
powerful weapon in the war against chauvinism, racism

and all manner of discrimination – that it is a mark, in fact, of what it means to be a civilised and progressive member of humankind in the twenty-first century. But with my Mr Grumpy hat on I might equally say that it is a joyless ideology which crushes dissent, glorifies victim-hood and special pleading, and stops children playing conkers. I am going to wimp out of this dilemma. This chapter is a history of the way other people have used the term rather than an attempt to say what I think it means myself. Feeble, I know, but there is good prece-dent for this kind of approach: one way of dealing with conflicting historical narratives (of the kind you find in the very different ways Palestinians and Israelis tell the story of the land they both claim, for example) is to explain each of them and let them stand against one another. This chapter is offered in that rather BBCish spirit.

To my surprise I have found no other attempt to produce an objective history of Political Correctness in recent writing on the subject – at least, if such a thing exists I have missed it in the course of my research. That may be because it is such an ideologically charged issue, and almost everyone who writes about it is doing polemics rather than research. But it could also be because the search for the origins of the PC phenomenon take one up some dauntingly dark avenues. The phrase 'politically correct' has become almost aggressively middle-brow, but the concept has emerged from really quite high-falutin' and abstruse academic arguments. My apologies in advance if this expedition involves trekking through some densely wooded intellectual thickets; I do not know what a Belgian deconstructionist looks like either, and I shall do my best not to get us too lost in the fog of war.

The first recorded use of the phrase 'politically correct' is a curiosity more than anything else; it appears in a 1792 judgement delivered by the Supreme Court of the United States. The state of Georgia was sued over non-payment for goods supplied during the then recent War of Independence with Britain, and the Supreme Court Justices of the day declared that a part of the evidence presented on Georgia's behalf was 'not politically correct' in the sense that it did not accurately reflect the political status of the United States at the time. The case had important implications for the relationship between the Federal Government in Washington and the individual states of the Union, and if you are a student of American constitutional law *Chisholm v. Georgia* will no doubt occupy a prominent drawer in your intellectual filing cabinet. For students of PC it falls into the 'interesting but useless' category of information.

But the modern history of the term also begins in the United States. Ruth Perry, a left-wing American academic and specialist in eighteenth-century English Literature, stakes the left-wing claim on its origins in her essay 'A Short History of the Term "Politically Correct"'. She argues that the seeds of PC-ness were sown in the New Left enthusiasm for Chairman Mao's *Little Red Book*, that publishing phenomenon of the 1960s. More than 900 million copies of *Quotations from Chairman Mao* – as it was more properly known in China – came into circulation, that staggering figure no doubt in part reflecting the fact that in the China of Mao's Cultural Revolution you were likely to be beaten up by the Red Guards if you were caught without one. When it was translated into English in 1966, *The Little Red Book* became a touchstone text for revolutionary groups like the Black Panthers in the United States; Mao's idea of a 'correct' ideological line came with it. As the first written example of 'politically correct' in its modern sense, Perry cites a piece, published in 1970 by the radical African American writer Toni Cade, on the link between racism and sexism: 'Racism and chauvinism are anti-people,' Cade wrote, 'and a man cannot be politically correct and a chauvinist too.'

But Ruth Perry also argues that from a very early stage the term was 'double-edged': 'no sooner was it invoked as a genuine standard for socio-political practice,' she says, '. . . than it was mocked as purist, ideologically rigid, and authoritarian.' As evidence for this she describes the debate which took place at the 'famous [not, I am afraid, to me] Barnard College Conference' held in 1982 on the question of whether there is such a thing as 'politically correct' sex; 'What was a feminist to do if her sexual gratification was tied to politically incorrect fantasies? Were antipornography activists simply re-inscribing Victorian values of prudish "good girls"? Was the "prosex" faction simply enacting patriarchal paradigms of domination and submission and playing into the hands of a billion dollar pornography industry that exploited and dehumanized women?' Abstruse and academic these matters may be – dry and dull they are not!

Perry tells this chapter in PC's story in such admirably neutral academic tones that it is difficult to work out whether she is being po-faced or writing with a smile on her lips, but I rather suspect (and certainly hope) that the latter is the case. The debate at the conference was apparently made all the more fractious by a 'Speakout on Politically Incorrect Sex' organised by the Lesbian Sex Mafia, 'self-identified S/M lesbian feminists who argue that the moralism of the radical feminists stigmatises sexual minorities such as butch/femme couples, sado-masochists, and man/boy lovers, thereby legitimizing "vanilla sex" lesbians and at the same time encouraging a return of a narrow, conservative, "feminine" vision of ideal sexuality'. 'Vanilla Sex' means vaginal intercourse for heterosexual couples, and for homosexuals 'sex that does not extend beyond affection, mutual masturbation, and oral and anal sex'. That definition was quoted in the *British Medical Journal* – just in case you thought I was getting carried away at this point.

The point of telling this story in some detail, Perry explains, is to make the case that 'Political Correctness' began as a kind of in-joke of the Left, with 'self-mocking, ironised meanings'. And – this is the crux of her polemic

– she declares herself infuriated by the way 'our own term of self-criticism' has been appropriated by the Right as a term of abuse. Because by the time she wrote her essay in 1992 the right-wing counter-offensive against PC was in full swing.

The first decisive moment in the right-wing narrative of PC's history was the winter of 1990/1; with a series of high-profile newspaper and magazine articles in the United States the concept of Political Correctness erupted into the public consciousness. *Newsweek* ran a cover story with the strap 'Watch What You Say. Thought Police'. Then the *New York Magazine* carried a piece asking 'Are you politically correct?' It was accompanied by a photo montage of book-burning Nazis and Red Guards parading the enemies of the Cultural Revolution, and it conjured a frightening genie from the PC bottle: 'an eclectic group; they include multiculturalists, feminists, radical homo-sexuals, Marxists, New Historicists' (they could have added the Vanilla Sex lot to the list if they had thought about it). 'What unites them,' said the magazine, '. . . is their conviction that Western culture and American society are thoroughly and hopelessly racist, sexist and oppressive.' There were pieces too in the *New York Times*, the *Atlantic*, the *New Republic* and the *Village Voice*.

The pieces tapped into a head of steam about what was happening on America's university campuses which had been building up since the mid 1980s. One of the odd things about revisiting the battlefields where these early

PC skirmishes were fought is that so many of the arguments centred around questions which in this country only really preoccupy the readers of *The Times Higher Educational Supplement*. The title of perhaps the best-known book which heralded the right-wing assault on PC in the United States provides a flavour of the somewhat specialist educational focus of their early polemics; Allan Bloom's *The Closing of the American Mind: How Higher Education has Failed Democracy and Impoverished the Souls of Today's Students* was a runaway success when it was published in 1987, proving, in the words of one critic, that 'it is possible to write an alarmist book about the state of higher education with a long-winded title and make a great deal of money'. The author, until then a relatively obscure philosophy don at the University of Chicago, enjoyed more than six months at the top of the *New York Times* bestseller list – surely beyond the wildest dreams of most academics. Looking down the contents page one does wonder why so many Americans forked out for this weighty tome (and, indeed, how many of them actually read it); there are chapters called things like 'The Nietzscheanization of the Left and Vice Versa', and 'From Socrates' *Apology* to Heidegger's *Rektoratsrede*'.

The book is learned, beautifully written and at times elegiac. But there is real hatred at its heart, and one cannot help the suspicion that that is what made it so popular. Here is Bloom on the eighties teenager:

Picture a thirteen-year-old boy sitting in the living room of his family home doing his math assignment while wearing his Walkman headphones or watching MTV. He enjoys the liberties hard won over centuries by the alliance of philosophic genius and political heroism, consecrated by the blood of martyrs; he is provided with comfort and leisure by the most productive economy ever known to mankind; science has penetrated the secrets of nature in order to provide him with the marvellous, lifelike electronic sound and image reproduction he is enjoying. And in what does progress culminate? A pubescent child whose body throbs with orgasmic rhythms; whose feelings are made articulate in hymns to the joys of onanism or the killing of parents; whose ambition is to win fame and wealth in imitating the drag queen who makes the music.

Those of us who are parents have all been irritated by slobby teenagers from time to time, but is this not, as they might say, 'going it a bit'?

More than anything else, Allan Bloom really, really hated the 1960s and everything they stood for. Clearly traumatised by his own experiences as a university don during the student rebellions of that turbulent decade, he accuses the university authorities of the time of a dereliction of moral duty comparable to that of the German intellectual class of the Nazi era:

The American university in the sixties was experiencing the same dismantling of the structure of rational inquiry as had the German

university in the thirties. No longer believing in their higher
vocation, both gave way to a highly ideologized student popu-
lace . . . Whether it be Nuremberg or Woodstock, the principle
is the same. As Hegel was said to have died in Germany in 1933,
Enlightenment in America came close to breathing its last during
the sixties.

No matter how elegantly written this may be, it is plainly
complete bollocks.

The fact that Bloom's book did so well despite the
manifest absurdity of such statements (and the almost
wilfully highbrow tone of some of the writing) tells us
something about American public opinion at the time:
people clearly felt that Something Was Up which they
did not like much. Quite what that Something was had
not really been articulated, but in Middle America's collective mind it was, in an ill-defined sort of way, connected
with the sixties, and it was being perpetrated on university campuses. The success of *The Closing of the American
Mind* generated a whole genre of polemics in a similar
vein. In 1991 *Illiberal Education: The Politics of Race
and Sex on Campus* by Dinesh D'Souza gave us the
wonderfully vivid phrase 'Visigoths in tweed' to describe
the academic vandals who were apparently doing such
terrible damage to America's national spirit. And another
gifted polemicist, Roger Kimball, weighed in with *Tenured
Radicals: How Politics has Corrupted our Higher
Education.*

Kimball is a journalist rather than an academic, and, despite that rather po-faced book title he was one of the first writers to have serious satirical fun at the expense of the PC brigade. In 1990 he attended the annual meeting of America's Modern Languages Association. 'Chicago's sobriquet, "the Windy City", seemed doubly appropriate at the end of December 1990,' he reported from the front line:

In addition to the frigid blasts, the snow, the icy rain, and the other seasonal vagaries that contribute to the city's festive spirit at that time of year, the Modern Languages Association convoked its 106th convention, filling . . . the halls and meeting rooms of the Hyatt Regency and other downtown hotels with gusts as chilling and impenetrable in their own way as any north wind barrelling off Lake Michigan.

Kimball uses the satirical technique of deadpan reporting to devastating effect; some of the best passages in the essay I am quoting simply list items on the convention programme:

There was session 692, arranged by the Marxist Literary Group, devoted to 'Gender, Race, and "Othering" in the Narrative Arts'. This panel was not, however, to be confused with number 26, 'The Poetics of "Othering": Gender, Class, and Cultural Identity in the Literature of Africa and its Diaspora', or with number 588, 'Reinventing Gender'. Other attractive sessions included number 62, 'The Other Captives: American Indian Oral Captivity Narratives', and number 590, 'The Ties that Bound: Homophobia and Relations among Males in Early America', in which one could hear papers on 'Sodomy in the New World', 'The Prurient Origins of the American Self', 'New English Sodom', and 'The Sodomitical Tourist'.

A few brave souls on the pro-PC side of the debate tried to answer humour with humour. A young English professor at the University of Illinois called Michael Bérubé published a piece in the trendy *Village Voice* magazine:

Thanks to our limited public image [he wrote archly], most folks now believe we brainwash our students by feeding them sixties radicalism alongside what one *New Republic* commentator calls 'warmed-over Nietzscheanism', thus turning them into *agents of political correctness* [his italics]. It's simple really; whenever my students hear me snap my fingers and quote Marx's eleventh thesis on Feuerbach, they spontaneously begin to decry sexism, racism, monologism, lookism, bagism, dragism and journalism.

Dead right, Michael – that is indeed what Middle America thought you and your ilk were up to, even if they had never heard of Feuerbach. It may have read like a good joke in Greenwich Village, but the tide of history was running the other way.

At some point in the course of these increasingly shrill polemics a bright young staffer in Republican Party headquarters must have woken up with a 'eureka' moment and asked what was becoming an increasingly obvious question: might there be a few votes to be had in this stuff? Because in May 1991, a couple of months after the big pieces on Political Correctness in *Newsweek* and the *New York Magazine*, George Bush ('Bush 41', that is, as opposed to his son, the 43rd president of the United States) made Political Correctness his target in a speech at the University of Michigan. The President painted this new-fangled phenomenon as a threat to all-American values: 'Ironically, on the 200th anniversary of our Bill of Rights,' he declared,

we find free speech under assault throughout the United States, including on some college campuses. The notion of political correctness has ignited controversy across the land. And although the movement arises from the laudable desire to sweep away the debris of racism and sexism and hatred, it replaces old prejudices with new ones. It declares certain topics off-limits, certain expression off-limits, even certain gestures off-limits.

The speech marked the moment when Political Correctness in the United States completed its journey from ivory tower to public forum. Bush had an enjoyably dotty record of letting his somewhat old-fashioned social notions show in his use of language; when he was running for a first term as president he explained away a poor performance in the Iowa Caucuses by saying that his supporters were 'busy on the golf course or at air shows or debutante parties', and he famously justified the invasion of Panama on the grounds that 'we cannot tolerate attacks on the wife of an American citizen'. But the Michigan speech sounded much more like calculated politics than a personal gripe. Connoisseurs of that period of American politics will remember that, despite his admirably responsible old-fashioned internationalism in foreign policy, George Bush senior was not above stirring up a bit of fear and loathing at home if he felt it would help him get votes. And he knew a good bogeyman when he saw one; several American commentators have remarked that a reversal of the letters PC gives you the initials of the Communist Party. The President, shortly to face a re-election campaign, pressed home his attack:

We should be alarmed at the rise of intolerance in our land and by the growing tendency to use intimidation rather than reason in settling disputes. Neighbours who disagree no longer settle matters over a cup of coffee. They hire lawyers, and they go to court. And political extremists roam the land, abusing the privilege of free speech, setting citizens against one another on the basis of class or race.

The image of 'political extremists' roaming the land has a certain pleasing New Frontier romance about it; one can imagine them riding into some tiny pioneer town and stirring up trouble between the neighbours like a bad cowboy in an old-fashioned Western. Whether the rather earnest-minded Eng. Lit. professors and researchers who had been the targets of most anti-PC rhetoric until then were really out and about – in their Visigothic tweed – engaged in such nefarious and subversive activities is another matter. But PC was now well and truly launched into national politics.

The Bush speech is also interesting because it reflects two characteristics of the PC World which we will encounter frequently on our journey. It is a recognition of the coincidence of the PC movement with the rise of the politics of identity ('setting citizens against one another on the basis of class or race'), and it is an example of the tendency to 'Christmas tree' the Political Correctness debate; strictly speaking, the phrase 'Christmas treeing' refers to an American congressional practice of 'tagging a host of special-interest amendments to a popular bill'; but it is a useful metaphor for the tendency to hang up all sorts of contemporary evils as baubles decorating the PC tree.

On this side of the Atlantic at the time of the Bush speech I suspect most of us saw Political Correctness as another illustration of the general wackiness of Americans. But something important was stirring on the Left here too. The early left-wing history of PC in Britain is rather well told in an essay by the social commentator Stuart Hall – Jamaican born, but a long-time resident of Britain.

Hall argues that PC arose from a need to find new

weapons to challenge the apparently eternal hegemony of wicked Thatcherite Tory rule. 'The rise of political correctness,' he wrote (this was in 1994), 'seems intimately connected with the fact that, in the US until recently, and in the UK still, the 1980s and 1990s have been marked by the political new right.' The intellectual triumph of right-wing free market economics – so the argument ran – had destroyed the old left-wing causes of class warfare and social justice, and the Left needed something to replace them. It found that, Hall argues, in individual liberation movements – for gay rights, for example – and the concept of Political Correctness was born in the process.

In the old days [he wrote], class and economic deprivation were what the left considered the 'principal contradiction' of social life. All the major social conflicts seemed to flow from and lead back to them. The era of PC is marked by the proliferation of the sites of social conflict to include conflicts around questions of race, gender, sexuality, the family, ethnicity and cultural difference, as well as issues around class and inequality . . . PC is also characteristic of the rise of 'identity politics', where shared social identity (as woman, Black, gay or lesbian), not material interest or collective disadvantage, is the mobilising factor.

It was an acute observation that has stood the test of time. Hall's analysis places the origins of our PC World firmly in the context of the political upheavals which followed the collapse of Communism and the end of the Cold War. The early 1990s saw a hugely important shift from the politics of ideology to the politics of identity, from a world where the critical question was 'What do I believe?' to one where that question was supplanted by 'Who am I?' The consequences of that are still with us, and those 'conflicts around questions of race, gender, sexuality, the family, ethnicity and cultural difference' are as live as ever – indeed, they are the subject of much of this book.

Come the general election of 1997, and the story of Political Correctness in Britain changed hands. With New Labour in power, it became the property of the Right, and anti-PC polemics came to provide a focus for right-wing protest against the status quo in just the way PC itself provided an outlet for the Left in the Thatcher–Major years. As a consequence, the 'Christmas-treeing' of the phenomenon became quite frenzied, and today all sorts of aspects of Blair–Brown Britain which make some sections of the population feel uneasy – 'nanny state' legislation in areas like smoking and drinking, the ''ealth and safety' culture, the mollycoddling of children and so on – are hung hotch-potch together on the PC tree.

A striking illustration of this process came obligingly to hand in the *Daily Telegraph* as I was writing this chapter. 'Health Watchdog Bans Hancock's Advice to Go to Work on an Egg' reads the headline. The piece reported that the egg industry had wanted to mark the fiftieth anniversary of Tony Hancock's 'Go to Work on an Egg' commercials by re-broadcasting them, but had been forbidden to do so by the Broadcast Advertising Clearance Centre on the grounds that an egg a day is not a 'varied diet'. 'Is this political correctness gone mad?' asked a box at the bottom of the piece; it invited readers to 'have your say' on the *Telegraph* website. It may indeed be mad, but is it, strictly speaking, 'Political Correctness'? Certainly not in the sense that America's cultural campus warriors or the campaigners against Vanilla Sex used the phrase – I do not think it was the sort of thing George Bush senior had in mind either, and although I have written a little about diet in Chapter 5, I am more interested in the PC dilemma posed by really delicious but dubious dishes like *foie gras* than I am in eggs.

No matter; a couple of days after the egg story appeared it provoked a really brilliant anti-PC Jeremiad about the state of modern Britain. Under the headline 'Alas Poor Britain. The Best Name for it is Absurdistan', Gerard Baker of *The Times* described the decision to ban the adverts as 'Stalinist' and asked, 'How long will it be before it is not just the free speech of advertising that is curtailed but the evil practice it promotes, and we ban egg consumption along with smoking?' Quite a long time would be my answer, but Baker is on a roll:

At the root of this nonsense is, of course, the sheer scale of government. The reason you can't be allowed to eat an egg is that, because of the lack of real choice in healthcare provision, you're no longer responsible for the financial consequences of your own actions. If you get heart disease from too much choles- terol, the State, collectively known as the NHS, will have to treat you; and that costs the State more and more money so the State will have to stop you from doing it in the first place.

Once off in this direction there is no stopping him; in a few brisk paragraphs he whisks through the malign influ- ence of the State on our universities, the debilitating size of the public sector workforce and its impact on our sense of responsibility, the absence of any resignations in the wake of the kidnapping of the British sailors and marines who were taken by the Iranians in the Gulf – quite a leap from an egg advertisement, that – and finally the iniqui- ties of the Blair negotiating strategy at the EU summit which was taking place in Brussels that weekend. Bracing stuff indeed.

And if that gets your pulses going, you will love this. It is from the writer Anthony Browne, in a pamphlet published by the think-tank Civitas in 2007: '. . . political correctness has now become the dominant ideology of the West . . . PC has completed a pretty clean sweep, imbedding itself through all the institutions, from school to TV broadcasts, from company HQs to the army. It is difficult to think of any part of life – certainly public life – that has not succumbed to the dictates of PC.' If that makes you want to emigrate to the United States, don't

– it's just as bad there apparently. Browne quotes Paul Weyrich's *Letter to Conservatives*, which offers a similarly alarming picture of the onward march of Political Correctness:

it is impossible to ignore the fact that the United States is becoming an ideological state. The ideology of Political Correctness, which openly calls for the destruction of our traditional culture, has so gripped the body politic, has so gripped our institutions, that it is even affecting the Church. It has completely taken over the academic community. It is now pervasive in the entertainment industry, and it threatens to control literally every aspect of our lives.

Hold on, chaps, time for a reality check.

Observant readers will remember that PC's history really got going in the 1980s – at least twenty years ago. That was when those Visigoths in Tweed began in earnest their work of corrupting the nation's youth, stuffing their heads with Political Correctness and killing their capacity for independent critical thinking – closing their minds and destroying their souls, in fact. The generation which went to university in the 1980s and early 1990s has now come of age; if you graduated in the year that Allan Bloom's book came out, for example, you would now be in your early forties.

If these nearly middle-aged men and women really had been so hopelessly brainwashed by a diet of left-wing propaganda when they were students, would the America that went to war in Afghanistan and Iraq and twice elected George Bush junior to the White House really be as it is? The generation that came of age then witnessed the end of the Cold War; many of them would have been at university during the Year of Revolutions, 1989, and however batty some of their professors may have been, the lessons of the fall of Soviet-style Communism cannot have been entirely lost on them. Do we look at America today and say that the best and the brightest of the forty-somethings have been irredeemably corrupted by the lefty nonsense they picked up at university? There are no doubt plenty of reasons to be rude about the United States of today, but the accusations that it is effete or run by a coalition of card-carrying commies and half-literate sixties-idolising swingers is surely not one of them. We shall need our bullshit-detectors on full alert during this journey.

Anthony Browne's pamphlet brings the PC story up to date, and I shall be returning to it later in this book, but before we end this chapter we must, I fear, deal briefly with those Belgian deconstructionists.

Paul Berman, the clever cultural commentator whose words I have quoted at the opening of this chapter, made a valiant effort in a 1992 essay to trace the philosophical origins of Political Correctness right back to the revolutionary spirit of 1968 and the structuralist and post-structuralist philosophers whose ideas were so much in vogue at the time – figures like Jacques Derrida,

Michel Foucault and Jacques Lacan. I have never really understood structuralism – let alone its 'post' variation – but I think I know enough about it to be sure that I do not like it. It is easy to have cheap fun at the expense of these characters and their disciples – and I look forward to doing so at some length in Chapter 5 – but their ideas do pop up in an insistent way from time to time in this story, and Berman's summary of their beliefs is quite helpful (although it would, I am sure, be dismissed by the men themselves as a disgraceful caricature). He writes:

if they had a single gist, it was this: Despite the claims of humanist thought, the individual is not free to make his own decision, nor is the world what it appears to be. Instead, we and the world are permeated by giant, hidden, impersonal structures, the way that human forms in *Invasion of the Body Snatchers* are inhabited by extraterrestrial beings . . . Mostly there was the idea that regardless of how the permeating structures are labelled, One Big Structure underlies all the others – and if this deepest of all structures can be described, it is by means of the linguistic theories that derive from Ferdinand de Saussure. That is: We are permeated by the structures of language. We imagine that language is our tool, but it is we who are the tool and language is our master.

To almost anyone who works with words, that last idea is of course anathema, and it may explain why suspicion of PC language runs so deep among my fellow broad-casters and journalists. We spend our time trying to make words the tools of meaning – perhaps, at the risk of sounding pompous, one might even say the tools of truth. We know that when we are lazy or do not care greatly about a story we fall easily into the 'structures' of jour-nalistic cliché, but that when we are working at our best what we write is distinctively our own because of the words we choose and the rhythms we give them. If we are fooling ourselves and we really do no more than reflect 'structures' over which we have no control, there would not seem to be much point in getting up in the morning – certainly not at three in the morning, which is the time of my alarm call for the *Today* programme.

Plainly there is more at stake here than words, and in the course of this book I am going to allow myself to roam promiscuously through the worlds of politics, culture, sociology, academia, morality and religion, food, drink and fun. But the importance of words is the one point on which both sides of the PC debate agree.

# 2

# Language in a PC World

In the beginning was the Word . . .

The Gospel of St John

When I tell someone that I am writing a book about Political Correctness the response usually runs along the lines of 'Humph. About time too – hope you're against it, obviously.' And usually this is followed by some robust comments about the way PC is corrupting our mother tongue.

For a while I thought this was simply a depressing reflection of the fact that I have reached the age when all my friends have old fart opinions, but when I began to get the same response chatting with interviewees on foreign assignments I decided there must be rather more to it than that. An Israeli intellectual, sitting in his local café which had once been the target of a suicide bomb attack, talked movingly and thoughtfully about the impact of the second *intifada* on the Jewish sense of identity – and then, in our informal chat once the micro-phones had been turned off, took off into something close to a rant when I mentioned the words 'Political Correctness'; it was, he felt, a dangerous and insidious influence on those precious choices writers can make about which words they use. If someone who lives with the daily realities of the bloody conflict between Israel and the Palestinians can get steamed up about this row, then who am I to talk it down?

So I am working on the assumption that if you are reading this book you probably feel instinctively that Political Correctness is a Bad Thing, and you want to find your judgement confirmed here. You may also be hoping you can take away a few extreme examples of ridiculous perversions of language in the name of Political Correctness with which to amuse your friends – that this book will be what the French call a *sottisier*, an extended version of those lists of idiocies like *Pseuds Corner* and *Colemanballs* that do so well in *Private Eye*. Let me propose a deal to you. I am going to find the most ridicu-lous example I can of linguistic prohibition on PC grounds – and then try to persuade you that it might be justified. If I can succeed in that, I ask you to accept the possi-bility that politically correct language just might, in certain circumstances, be a force for good rather than the reverse. If I fail, give up with this book and place it – in the inter-ests of a politically correct cause – in the recycling bin.

The competition for the most ludicrous PC excess is

tough. Typing the phrase 'Political Correctness gone mad' into the internet search engine Google produced well over a million answers. There were some strong contenders from various British government agencies and quangos; 'bedlam' was apparently considered an inappropriate word for civil servants by the Welsh Development Agency because it was the name of Britain's first lunatic asylum, bulldozer once meant a man employed to beat slaves, and if you talk about a 'manila' envelope (an item with which one imagines civil servants are more familiar than most of us) you are, it seems, not describing its colour but making a reference to 'a bangle used to buy slaves'. 'Dutch courage' might imply that the people of the Netherlands need a drink before going into battle – most people probably do if they are at all sane – and, most intriguingly, 'maverick' could be offensive to people from countries where cows are considered holy: the term owes its origin to Samuel Maverick, a nineteenth-century cattle rancher from Texas who defied authority by refusing to brand his cattle.

America, of course, had plenty to offer too, my favourite being the case of the white Washington bureaucrat who was fired for using the word 'niggardly' in a meeting. One of those present is said to have asked, 'Do you really think he didn't notice he had to pass "nigger" before he could get to the "dly"?' I also enjoyed the story, reported in the *Guardian*, that the *Fresno Bee*, a Californian newspaper, had to publish a correction after referring to 'a plan for putting Massachusetts back into the African-American';

the piece should have read 'back into the black' (and of course there was the pleasurable irony of this particular story appearing in the *Grauniad*, with its own tradition of humorous typos).

In the end, however, I settled on the following item from our very own BBC website, dated Friday 17 May 2002:

## Talking point: has political correctness gone mad?

Home Office minister John Denham has been criticised by the police for using the phrase 'nitty gritty' because of race relations rules.

Mr Denham used the phrase during a debate at the Police Federation conference in Bournemouth.

He was told that police officers could face disciplinary charges for saying 'nitty-gritty' because it dates from the slavery era.

The theory was that the term had originally been used to describe the debris left in the hold of a slaving ship which had delivered its cargo to the Americas – a mixture of human parasites (the expression 'nit-picking' was discouraged for similar reasons) and human waste which, after a journey across the Atlantic of several weeks without any sanitation, would have been unimaginably vile.

The problem with this etymology is that there is no

evidence of the phrase 'nitty-gritty' being written down until the 1950s. My *Dictionary of Slang* tells me that it is 'US Black, 1950+, ety[mology] unknown'. The slave trade was abolished in 1807 and it seems extremely unlikely that a phrase like that would have survived for a hundred and fifty years purely by word of mouth, without ever being recorded. So we have what appears to be the perfect PC atrocity. Not only is it completely absurd, but it is based on a fallacy. A useful and rather vivid expression, used without malice or prejudice, has been condemned for entirely spurious reasons. I also found the John Denham incident cited as an example of 'Victimocracy' in *We're (Nearly) All Victims Now!*, an anti-PC pamphlet published by David Green of the right-wing think-tank Civitas in 2006, which confirmed my view that it makes a good test case.

I will now try to persuade you that it is not as straightforward as it seems.

As my main witness I call a writer not generally associated with the Political Correctness movement. Ezra Pound was almost obsessively passionate about the way language is used and understood. He wrote books and essays with titles like 'The ABC of Reading' and 'How to Read', and they are full of quotable gobbets about the power of language and good writing: 'It is as important for the purpose of thought to keep language efficient as it is in surgery to keep tetanus bacilli out of one's bandages' and 'The man of understanding can no more sit quiet and resigned while his country lets its literature decay, and lets good writing meet with contempt, than a good doctor should sit quiet and contented while some ignorant child was infecting itself with tuberculosis under the impression that it was merely eating jam tarts.' Once he gets into his stride he reveals some of the attitudes which would get him into serious trouble today: 'A people that grows accustomed to sloppy writing is a people in process of losing grip on its empire.' And, with what one can only describe as deplorable animalism, he has this to say about the enemies of literature: 'They regard it as dangerous, chaotic, subversive. They try every idiotic and degrading wheeze to tame it down. They try to make a bog, a marasmus, a great putridity in place of sane and active ebullience. And they do this from sheer simian and pig-like stupidity, and from a failure to understand the function of letters.' Poor old pigs and apes – they are, as we know, in fact both rather clever animals. This is high-octane grumpy-old-mandom.

I studied Pound's translations from Latin and Chinese while I was at university; it is wonderful poetry – in contrast to the much more famous *Cantos* which I have always found baffling and tiresome – and I still read bits of it today. During a recent house move I discovered the dissertation on the subject I wrote for my finals in a box full of old papers; I could not understand a single sentence I wrote all those years ago. Either I was terribly clever in those days, before years of broadcast journalism addled my brain, or I had learnt to write in the approved academic jargon of the day and have since, mercifully, forgotten it all. But I still have very vivid memories of some of Pound's ideas and passages of his writing.

Pound believed that all written language has its origins in pictures, and that the best poetry was made by drawing on the reserve of concrete images which words still contain. He based many of his ideas on the work of Ernest Fenollosa, an American scholar who taught at the University of Tokyo in the late nineteenth century; making the rather obvious point that some Chinese characters look like images of the object they represent – the characters for 'man' and 'tree', for example, are indeed like stylised sketches – Fenollosa argued that Chinese characters are 'abbreviated pictures' and, as Pound summed it up, that 'Chinese ideogram does not try to be the picture of a sound, or to be a written sign recalling a sound, but it is still the picture of the thing'. 'Fenollosa,' Pound writes, 'was telling how and why language written in this way HAD TO STAY POETIC; simply couldn't help being and staying poetic in a way that a column of English type might very well not stay poetic.'

Fenollosa was writing at a time when Western understanding of East Asian cultures was at an early stage – his tenure in Tokyo was not so very long after the end of the extraordinary period of self-imposed isolation which cut Japan off from the rest of the world – and some of his ideas are today regarded as every bit as dodgy as the etymology of 'nitty-gritty' I have quoted above. But in a way that does not matter. Because when his widow passed on his notes and unpublished essays to Ezra Pound she gave the young poet the key to his particular poetic gift: the power to mint metaphors which change the way you see the world for ever. You can see Fenollosa's influence directly in what is perhaps Pound's most famous short poem, the *haiku* 'In a Station at the Metro', which he wrote in 1916:

> The apparition of these faces in the crowd
> Petals on a wet, black bough.

Once you have read that it is, I think, impossible to stop the image popping into your head from time to time while waiting for the tube, or walking down a crowded Oxford Street.

I am still haunted by Pound's reflection on the classical Greek word *glaukos* which I read, appropriately, on holiday on a Greek island while still a student. It crops up many times in Homer, whom Pound admired more than almost any other poet, and there is some dispute about whether it means 'grey-green' or 'silvery-flashing'. Pound argues that it comes from the leafage of an olive tree in the wind, which 'does not glare but glitters, the pale under-face of the leaves alternating with that dark-upper face'. So when you describe the sea as 'grey-green' you are really saying that it looks like a grove of ruffled olive trees. Was Pound right? Probably not. But does it matter? I have long since lost my close interest in Greek etymology, but when someone talks about a grey-green sea, the image of an olive grove glittering in the Ionian breeze comes immediately into my mind.

It can be awkward reading Ezra Pound. During the Second World War he was based in Italy and acted as a propagandist for the Axis powers – he escaped a treason trial in the United States on the grounds of insanity. You feel that he is someone with an instinctive grasp of the way language works, yet every so often you get a sense of some of his dangerous ideas about race – he was undoubtedly anti-Semitic – pushing their way to the surface: 'Different climates and different bloods have different needs, different spontaneities, different reluctances, different ratios between different groups of impulse and unwillingness, different constructions of throat, and all these leave trace in the language, and leave it more ready and unready for certain communications and registrations.' If talk of 'different bloods' makes you squirm a bit, this, a page later, is surely true: 'There is no end to the number of qualities which some people can associate with a given word or kind of word, and most of these vary with the individual.'

Which brings me back to 'nitty-gritty'. After reflecting a little on John Denham's difficulties at the Police Federation I realised that I have in fact seen this (theoretical) substance myself, or at least something very like it.

When I was a teenager my family lived in the West African country of Ghana, and we were taken to see the coastal forts of Elmina and Cape Coast. These were the embarkation points for slaves on their journey to the Americas, and the sense of pathos that hangs about their walls is magnified by the extraordinary beauty of the stretch of coastline on which they lie. At Cape Coast there is a tunnel leading from the cells, where the slaves were held, to the beach where longboats waited to row them out to the waiting slaving ships, and as you step out of the darkness you see – a last look at Africa for them – nothing but palm trees, white sand, sea and sky. The Castle also has a telling monument to Christian hypocrisy; there is a neat little white-washed Anglican chapel perched in the centre of the courtyard – just above the main entrances to the slave cells.

But by far the most effective illustration of Cape Coast's shameful history is a simple cut in the floor of one of these dreadful dark dungeons. There was, of course, no sanitation for the cargo of human beings who waited – sometimes for several weeks and in tropical heat – in these pits. Their faeces gradually formed a crust which, over time, raised the floor level. When someone died, and many did, the slave traders did not generally trouble to remove the corpse, so the mix was enriched by human remains. To bring home what this meant, the Ghanaian tourist authorities hacked through the encrustation to the original floor, leaving an exposed face on view.

The depth is some eighteen inches – eighteen inches of packed and congealed human misery. I still have a vivid memory of how shocking I found this as a boy. What was this dreadful substance called? Almost certainly not 'nitty-gritty', as I have argued earlier, but now that the substance and the word are linked in my mind I suspect I shall be just that little bit more reluctant to use it than I was before. It will be very difficult to 'un-think' that connection, not least because the thing-that-is-probably-not-called-nitty-gritty had such a strong impact on me; my teenage experience has joined Ezra Pound's list of the 'number of qualities' which I associate with this particular expression.

Convinced? I have probably not made quite the case I promised at the beginning of this chapter, and of course this falls some considerable way short of an argument for condemning the unfortunate Mr Denham for what he said to the Police Federation. But it is a way of making a case for the unpredictable power of words. They can act like an unstable chemical mix or a cluster bomb – even apparently innocent expressions can be full of associations and meanings liable to blow up when you least expect it. And when that happens, when, for example, some incident brings a hidden meaning alive, it can and should change the way we speak. The Washington-based English writer Christopher Hitchens was one of the earliest and most vociferous opponents of the PC movement – polemic is his stock-in-trade and he does it very well. But even he admits, in an anti-PC piece he wrote in the early 1990s, that 'Because of an adored friend with chronic MS, I myself stopped employing that *New Left Review* perennial "sclerotic" to describe petrified institutions like the British monarchy.' The champions of Political Correctness are often accused of being the enemies of language; in fact, as I shall argue later in this chapter, they pay it the greatest imaginable compliment, because their creed is a recognition of the complexity of the way it works.

Even words that are very well known in this context can carry more meanings than we imagine. We all know that the sensitivity about the 'n-word' derives from its association with slavery. But many of you reading this will not be aware of how deeply embedded it once was in American slang. The *Cassell Dictionary of Slang* (I am using a 1998 edition) lists no fewer than ninety-five compounds and phrases formed from the 'nigger' root. Thus 'niggamation; *n* (19C) the speeding up of automobile production lines, on which the bulk of workers are African Americans, which gets more cars built but does not require the company to pay any more wages'. Thus 'nigger and halitosis' to mean liver and onions – that one was coined as recently as the 1940s. Or 'niggeritis; *n* (20C) the urge to lie down and take a nap after a heavy meal'. And so it goes on. And on – a vast verbal constellation of nastiness built around that single word. No wonder it provokes such strong feelings.

Words and phrases can, conversely, sometimes have hidden meanings which remain dormant even when they have indisputable etymological pedigrees. I was on the point of using the expression 'beyond the pale' in the paragraph above but checked myself to investigate its origins – linguistic self-examination becomes an irresistible tic when one is writing this kind of thing. It turns out that it, too, has rather nasty connotations. The 'pale' was originally nothing more than a safe area enclosed by a paling fence – so to be 'beyond the pale' was to be outside the area accepted as 'home'. No problem with that, but in 1791 Catherine the Great created a 'Pale of Settlement' in Russia – a western border region of the country in which Jews were allowed to live; a sort of ghetto, in fact. Some Jews were allowed to live 'beyond the pale' as a concession, but the idea was to restrict trade between Jews and native Russians – and pales were enforced in other European countries too. So the expression 'beyond the pale' has its roots in the great crime of European anti-Semitism, and yet is routinely used without any sense of the weight it carries. There are, it seems, no fixed rules here.

As a guide through this maze I would like to propose our English Springer Spaniel puppy, a recent addition to the household at the time of writing. While we awaited his arrival – dog lovers will know that puppies must remain with their mothers for a minimum of eight weeks – a family battle of surprisingly ferocity was fought over his name. At an early stage I suggested 'Truffle', but road-testing at my teenage step-daughter's school revealed that several other pupils had dogs of that name, and it was abandoned on the grounds of a lack of originality. This unleashed a furious tit-for-tat of proposal and counter-proposal between my step-daughter and my daughter, names flashing back and forth like an exchange of machine-gun fire. Literature was ransacked for suitable figures – 'Gatsby', 'Bilbo Baggins' – and my wife's old Hausa dictionary was scoured for something exotic-sounding ('Aminci', meaning friendship, had too many syllables and 'Iska', the wind, was a little feminine for a male dog). My younger son, on his gap year somewhere in the Amazon rainforest, occasionally sent facetious suggestions via the internet – 'I met a lovely Brazilian girl who called herself Madam FruFru – any chance of pitching that to the board?' or simply 'Meat-flaps' being examples of the kind of unhelpful ideas we found waiting in our Facebook inboxes. The elder son was superior ('Psmith with a silent P?') and more upmarket ideas floated in from time to time from his girlfriend ('Truman' and 'Benedict' among them). The breeder suggested 'Buddha' – he said the puppy showed signs of gentleness and placidity – but it was thought that shouting 'Buddha, stop that at once!' in the park might cause offence.

In the end we settled – amicably, but you may think, eccentrically – on 'Kudu', on the grounds that, like the African antelope of that name, he was large and full of spring. But I was left with a strong suspicion that behind the passion which informed the Battle of the Names lay an instinctive sense of the link between naming and power. When God gave man dominion over animals the book of Genesis records it thus: 'Then the Lord God said, "It is not right that the man should be alone . . ." So out of the ground the Lord God formed every animal of the field and every bird of the air, and brought them to the man to see what he would call them; and whatever the man called each living creature, that was his name.' When you name a person or a thing you are asserting a hierarchical relationship and your rights of possession.

Modern politicians are taught this ancient truth in media school; on the *Today* programme men and women I have never met – far less consider friends – regularly address me by my Christian name because it creates a sense that they are 'in control' of the interview. Sometimes I find that I am being addressed in this familiar way by people I would not even recognise in the street – many politicians prefer to be interviewed from Westminster or one of our radio cars rather than make the journey out to the BBC studios in White City, and because of the odd sleeping hours dictated by *Today* programme shifts I do not watch a huge amount of television. I find this intensely irritating. John Prescott, with whom I had a somewhat fractious on-air relationship (and, I should perhaps add, no off-air relationship at all) during his time as deputy prime minister once called me 'Eddie', and I am perfectly sure that he did it purely to annoy, safe in the knowledge that if I were to fire back a jaunty 'Johnny' I might lose my job.

There is a modern school of the philosophy of names known as 'nominalism'. With characteristic philosophical perversity, it argues precisely the reverse of what the term suggests. Nominalism is defined as 'the doctrine holding that abstract concepts, general terms or universals have no independent existence but exist only as names' and a 'philosophical position that various objects labelled by the same term have nothing in common but their name'. But our daily experience tells us that this is not true – or at least that it is not the way we perceive and use names, which is all that really matters. If you call your child Darren, or Marmaduke, or Fifi Trixibelle, you are making a statement; it seems unlikely that there are very many Darrens growing up with nannies in the nurseries of stately homes, or Marmadukes roughing it in the 1960s council estates in my part of south London – there may, of course, be Fifi Trixibelles in both, since that is a celebrity name that transcends class divisions. When we are told that 'all that two red things have in common is either a certain resemblance to each other or else, according to extreme nominalists, just the name red', we know that these extreme nominalists are – like most extremists – talking nonsense. It is probably true that in Plato's Cave there are no Ideal Forms of Darrenness, Marmadukeness or Fifi Trixibelleness casting their shadows on the wall, but if we meet anyone with any of these names our response to them is likely to be conditioned, in some degree at least, by general social and cultural assumptions about what the names convey.

So I propose the following as a general principle of Best Practice in Political Correctness: everyone should be able to decide for themselves what they are called. Let us call it the Kudu Principle in recognition of the role of the spaniel (which did not, of course, have this right) in developing the argument. It would be a statement of social democracy in the truest sense of the term – a reflection of the steady empowerment of the individual which Britain has witnessed over the past three or four decades. Why should we not accept people at the estimation they place upon themselves? Surely it is reasonable that, for example, someone who has lost a leg should ask to be called 'disabled' rather than being bundled up anonymously by the dismissive definite article which gives us 'the disabled'? That someone with a strong family memory of what it means to be called by the n-word should ask to be called African American instead (that is, after all, an accurate description of their heritage)? Or that someone attracted to members of the same sex should object to being called 'queer' and prefer the word 'gay'?

The Australian cultural critic Robert Hughes, in an especially shrill passage of his attack on Political Correctness in his 1993 book *The Culture of Complaint*, writes, 'We want to create a sort of linguistic Lourdes, where evil and

misfortune are dispelled by a dip in the waters of euphemism . . . Does the homosexual suppose that others love him
more or hate him less because he is called "gay" – that
term revived from eighteenth-century English slang, which
implied prostitution and living on one's wits?' Leaving aside
the intriguing but tendentious etymology, the answer to
that question must surely be 'yes', because at the very least
the use of the term represents an acceptance of his right
to decide how he would like to be known. The use of
politically correct language is, at its best, arguably no more
than an extension of that most British of virtues, good
manners: a recognition that one should always take the
feelings of others into consideration.

Hughes is similarly sceptical about the prohibition of
the n-word in the United States:

Seventy years ago, in polite white usage, blacks were called
'coloured people'. Then they became 'negroes'. Then 'blacks'.
Now 'African-Americans' or 'persons of colour' again. But for
millions of white Americans, from the time of George Wallace
to that of David Duke, they stayed niggers, and the shift of
names has not altered the facts of racism, any more than the
ritual announcement of Five-Year Plans and Great Leaps
Forward have turned the social disasters of Stalinism and Maoism
into triumphs.

For all its rhetorical gusto, that statement is simply untrue;
of course it has made a difference that the kind of

unpleasant nigger-related expressions I have given a flavour of earlier in this chapter are no longer part of everyday white American discourse. One of PC's champions has described it as 'placing emphasis on civility, the simple virtue of not giving offence'; a simple virtue it may be, but it is also one of the most essential to the smooth working of a free society.

Working in daily news programmes for an establishment institution like the BBC means that I face the tension between traditional and contemporary social attitudes in this area almost every day. Many members of the House of Lords, for example, now hate being given their titles. Whenever we interview Paddy Ashdown he insists that he should not be called 'Lord Ashdown' – but I know that if I called him 'Mr Ashdown' I would get a torrent of letters telling me that as a BBC presenter I should know better. Some Labour peeresses dislike being called 'Lady' X or Y, and ask you to use 'Baroness' instead. But no one would address a Baron as 'Baron' (life peer or not), so why should one call a Baroness 'Baroness'? The Kudu Principle gets round all this by giving the views of the individual greater weight than the rules laid out in books of Correct Form.

I once heard the Order of Precedence recited on stage as a comic turn. The Order, as its name suggests, dictates the way in which members of the British upper classes should 'process' on formal occasions. It stretches at unimaginable length from the Royal Family right down to 'Younger Sons of Younger Sons of Peers, Baronets' Younger Sons, Younger Sons of Knights in the same order as their Fathers, Naval, Military, Air and other Esquires by Office'. On the way down we meet all sorts of Gilbert and Sullivan-sounding characters (what, pray, is a 'Viceregent in Spirituals'?), we find that the Lord Chamberlain takes precedence over the other four Officers of State, but only when he is on duty, and we learn that 'Eldest Sons of Dukes of Blood Royal' come just above 'The five above State Officers if Marquesses, Marquesses, in the same order as Dukes, Dukes' Eldest Sons, the five above State Officers if Earls, Earls, in the same order as Dukes, Younger Sons of Dukes of Blood Royal, Marquesses' Eldest Sons, Dukes' Younger Sons . . .' and so on. You get the point. It does not sound obviously funny, but by the time we reached the foothills of this social mountain the audience was in stitches. And there was, of course, a political and social point being made. How much more egalitarian it is to live in a world where Political Correctness is more important than Correct Form, where good manners – in the deepest sense of the phrase – take precedence over etiquette.

But what if we actually want to be bad-mannered? If we actually want to insult someone? There are surely circumstances when this may be a perfectly reasonable thing to do. Take this passage from the *Daily Telegraph* art critic Richard Dorment; the target of his abuse was the latest piece of shock-art created by Damien Hirst, a skull encrusted with diamonds for which the artist was asking £50 million.

If anyone but Hirst had made this curious object, we would be struck by its vulgarity. It looks like the kind of thing Asprey or Harrods might sell to credulous visitors from the oil states with unlimited amounts of money to spend, little taste and no knowledge of art. I can imagine it gracing the drawing room of some African dictator or Colombian drug baron.

Hirst's whole appeal is based on insulting and outraging our sensibilities (the outrageous price tag he suggested for his 'curious object' was, one assumes, part of the joke in this case). This makes him part of a respectable artistic tradition, going back at least as far as the nineteenth-century French poet Baudelaire with his determination to '*epater le bourgeois*' (scandalise middle-class taste, or, as my elderly French–English dictionary rather charmingly puts it, 'startle the old fogeys'), but it does rather invite insult and outrage in return. Dorment's vituperative review seems deliberately cast in terms which are likely to annoy his target, and in that sense it is cleverly done. But in the process of insulting Hirst's *oeuvre* he manages to insult all sorts of other people too. In fact, the amount of collateral damage inflicted in such a short passage is quite remarkable; Dorment cheerfully dumps his tonnage of stereotyping on the Middle East, Latin America and Africa, and even people who shop at Asprey's and Harrods take flak too.

The passage is about as un-politically correct as it is possible to be, and it quite deliberately undermines the foundation of the Kudu Principle I have described above: Dorment is explicitly *rejecting* Hirst's right to be taken at his own estimation.

Could Dorment have been as insulting to Hirst as he wanted to be without insulting lots of other people too? Almost certainly not. Is that sort of writing acceptable? The logic of Political Correctness says no; common sense says it absolutely is. In reality, I suspect that this is one of those areas where people make instinctive and not entirely logical distinctions about where something like that appears; the tone would not sit very comfortably on the paper's news pages, but most *Telegraph* readers are probably perfectly happy to enjoy invective from a critic – after all, if critics cannot criticise it is difficult to see the point of them, and if they cannot be rude they are likely to be rather dull.

But once you begin asking questions like that, all sorts of mystifying genies pop their corks. What, for example, do you do when someone wants to be called by a name which falsifies reality? For someone who has lost a leg to be called 'differently abled' rather than 'disabled' is surely a misrepresentation of the truth. What about those phrases which by aiming at Political Correctness actually denigrate those they seek to protect? To say someone is 'short' is descriptive, nothing more, but to say they are 'vertically challenged' implies that their

shortness is a problem (although I have to confess I
have never actually come across an example of anyone
using the phrase 'vertically challenged' in a non-ironic
way). What about words that are given a new meaning
for PC reasons? I admit to a particular problem in this
regard with the use of the word 'chair' instead of
'chairman'. Plainly, a woman who chairs, say, a parliamentary committee or the board of a big company has
perfectly legitimate cause to wish to be called something other than 'chairman', but I still find myself
baulking at the application of a word which means a
piece of furniture to a human being. In 2007 Jack Straw,
as Leader of the Commons, decreed that 'chair' should
replace 'chairman' in all parliamentary business. The
formidable Tory MP Ann Widdecombe responded in
characteristically robust manner: 'Jack Straw is a silly
ass. A chair is a piece of furniture. It is not a person. I
am not a chair, because no one has ever sat on me.'
Leaving aside the temptation to speculate about what
it would be like to sit on Ann Widdecombe (I know
what it is like to be sat upon *by* her, because she has
done it to me quite often on the *Today* programme), I
have some sympathy with her basic point. 'Chairperson'
is not bad, but does not quite do it; an editorial in the
*New York Times* in 1991 asked 'Should *chairperson*, a
corrective for chairman, now be re-revised to *chairper-
daughter*?' Since I work on a daily news programme,
the issue comes up quite regularly for me and, in a

thoroughly pusillanimous manner, I usually try to fudge it by using the verb instead of the noun.

And then there are the words that have gone through so many changes that it leaves most of us dizzy. The first uses of the word 'gay' to mean homosexual can be traced to the 1920s and 1930s in the works of Noël Coward and Gertrude Stein, among others (the connotation of loose-living and promiscuity has always been there, although whether it was quite as specific as Robert Hughes suggests in the passage I have quoted above I rather doubt). But until at least the middle of the twentieth century the original meaning of 'gay' – the carefree spirit of a debutante cocktail party or a glamorous Hussar riding into battle – was still widely accepted. In the 1970s I can remember members of my parents' generation moaning that a 'perfectly good word' had been appropriated by homosexuals, but by the 1980s and certainly the 1990s most people had accepted that it was wrong to call people 'queer' because of their sexual orientation, and 'gay' had become well established in its modern meaning. Today I find that among my children's generation 'gay' has come to mean 'sad', as in 'that's so gay'. So in less than a hundred years the word has undergone a complete reversal.

Lurking behind all those questions are some much bigger ones: who owns words, and who can decide how they are used? Deborah Cameron, a teacher in linguistics, offered the following judgement in her essay 'Words, Words, Words': ' "Nigger" and "queer" obviously have a different value used by an East End skinhead and by the performers of Niggas with Attitude, or the performers of Queer Nation.' I know what she means, but I am not sure it is quite as obvious as she suggests. Of course, there is a difference between using a word in an offensive or abusive manner and using it with irony, but it remains the same word, and both the skinhead and the performers must agree on at least some of its meanings. If they do not, then they lose any possibility at all of communicating with one another – even in a hostile manner. Cameron was writing fifteen years ago; since then we have developed an orthodoxy which dictates that it is acceptable for black rap artists to use the n-word, but completely forbidden for a white person to do so. It is almost as if white people have in some way forfeited their linguistic rights because of the way our ancestors deprived black people of their much more basic rights in times gone by.

The contradictions in the current orthodoxy were brought into relief – in a rather tawdry sort of way – by a briefly notorious incident on the Channel 4 programme *Big Brother*. Here is the way it was described by Rod Liddle, my old boss on the *Today* programme, in his *Sunday Times* column.

When is it socially acceptable to call someone a 'nigger'? This is the question I posed to my posse of bitches and hos yesterday morning, in the wake of the latest Big Brother race row.

A fairly dense white woman, Emily Parr, was kicked off the programme for saying to her black housemate: 'You pushing it out, you nigger?'

It was perfectly acceptable, I was told, if the person committing the niggering is black, in which case it is meant as an affectionate soubriquet signifying ironic solidarity.

However, it should always be spelled with an 'a' and without asterisks. The plural form usually takes a 'z'.

What if a white woman says it, I asked. Ah, I was told, that's okay only if the white woman is a 'wigga', which is to say a white person habituated to using black vernacular and Jamaican slang to the extent that they cannot themselves remember what colour they are. These are confusing times and it is important to sort stuff like this out, to avoid giving possible offence.

A few months later the apparently never-ending saga of the 'n' word took yet another twist. A prominent black comedian and movie star, Eddie Griffin, suffered the indignity of his microphone being switched off when he used it on stage in Miami. The decision was taken by the sponsors of the event, the magazine *Black Enterprise*, when, ten minutes into his act, Griffin asked, 'Why are some black leaders telling us to stop using the n-word?' – he had, as the *Guardian* told the story, 'liberally peppered his jokes with the word'. The publisher of *Black Enterprise*, Earl Graves, received a standing ovation when he went on stage to denounce

Griffin: 'We will not allow our culture to go backwards. *Black Enterprise* stands for decency, black culture and dignity.'

The incident drew attention to the movement – spearheaded by, among others, the New York campaigner Al Sharpton – to reverse the growing acceptability of the word as a kind of post-modernist joke. The venerable American civil rights organisation, the National Association for the Advancement of Colored People, held a mock funeral for the word in the summer of 2007, and a slickly designed website was created to 'abolishtheword.com'. Its introduction offers a series of not-at-all-funny photographs of lynchings to the sound of the classic anti-racist song 'Strange Fruit': 'What's more powerful than a locomotive, faster than a speeding bullet, yet lighter than a feather and heavier than a raindrop?' asks its manifesto statement. 'The answer: Words.'

Confusing times indeed, and the Kudu Principle will not, I fear, suffice. For further guidance I shall turn to that Great Guru on matters linguistic, George Orwell.

Orwell's essay 'Politics and the English Language' has had an influence out of all proportion to its modest length (some fifteen pages in the edition I am using). I have a particular affection for it because of one of the examples of bad writing he quotes – it is taken from a letter to the left-wing journal *Tribune*:

If a new spirit is to be infused into this old country, there is
one thorny and contentious reform which must be tackled, and
that is the humanization and galvanization of the BBC. Timidity
here will bespeak cancer and atrophy of the soul. The heart of
Britain may be sound and of strong beat, for instance, but the
British lion's roar at present is like that of Bottom in
Shakespeare's *Midsummer Night's Dream* – as gentle as any
sucking dove. A virile new Britain cannot continue indefinitely
to be traduced in the eyes or rather ears, of the world by the
effete languors of Langham Place, brazenly masquerading as
standard 'English'. When the Voice of Britain is heard at nine
o'clock, better far and infinitely less ludicrous to hear aitches
honestly dropped than the present priggish, inflated, inhibited
school-ma'amish arch braying of blameless bashful mewing
maidens!

Having once been the target of a press campaign for
having a voice that was judged too 'posh' for the *Today*
programme, I take great comfort from the fact that similar
accusations were being bruited abroad in the 1940s – and
even more comfort from what I fondly imagine to be the
posthumous support of such a distinguished commentator. Orwell says of this passage that 'words and meaning
have almost parted company'.

The influence of Orwell's essay can be credited to his
remarkable ability – famously, of course, demonstrated in
the novel *1984* – to predict the curses which would afflict
future generations. Thus, for example, his translation of

a well-known passage from the Old Testament book of Ecclesiastes into 'modern English'. The original – in the King James version – reads like this:

I returned and saw under the sun, that the race is not for the swift, nor the battle to the strong, neither yet bread to the wise, nor yet riches to men of understanding, nor yet favour to men of skill; but time and chance happeneth to them all.

Orwell's modern English version comes out like this:

Objective considerations of contemporary phenomena compels the conclusion that success or failure in competitive activities exhibits no tendency to be commensurate with innate capacity, but that a considerable element of the unpredictable must invariably be taken into account.

Newspapers today are still having fun with exactly this kind of parody; it has, in fact, almost become institutionalised as a popular perennial (at the time of writing, the *Daily Telegraph* has just devoted a whole page to some particularly good examples inspired by its columnist Christopher Howse) and in my experience the genre seldom fails to amuse.

And long before the phrase 'collateral damage' became a shameful symbol of the spin-doctor's trick of wrapping nasty truths in euphemism, Orwell aimed this barb at the fellow-travelling academics who stuck up for Stalinism in the 1940s:

Consider for instance some comfortable English professor defending Russian totalitarianism. He cannot say outright, 'I believe in killing off your opponents when you can get good results by doing so.' Probably, therefore, he will say something like this: 'While freely conceding that the Soviet regime exhibits certain features which the humanitarian may be inclined to deplore, we must, I think, agree that a certain curtailment of the right to political opposition is an unavoidable concomitant of transitional periods, and that the rigours which the Russian people have been called upon to undergo have been amply justi-fied in the sphere of concrete achievement.'

The essay also anticipates the dangers of Political Correctness; Orwell observes that 'political' writing is usually bad writing, and that exceptions to this rule gener-ally occur when 'the writer is some kind of rebel, expressing his private opinions and not a "party line"'. His antidote to this echoes some of Ezra Pound's ideas about the importance of keeping language 'efficient'.

What is above all needed is to let the meaning choose the word, and not the other way about. In prose, the worst thing one can do with words is surrender to them . . . Probably it is better to put off using words as long as possible and get one's meaning as clear as one can through pictures and sensations. Afterwards one can choose, not simply *accept*, the phrases that will best cover the meaning, and then switch round and decide what impression one's words are likely to make on another person.

There is a huge amount of very good sense crammed into this short passage. Orwell recognises that it is important to think about the impact your words will have on other people; he says that this 'effort of the mind' will lead you to cut out 'all staler mixed images, all prefabricated phrases, needless repetitions, and humbug and vagueness generally'. The injunction also covers both the broad Kudu Principle of civility and the need to be alive to the baggage of a word's associations which Pound writes about. But all that comes second to meaning, which must always, always and without exception (and he is explicitly talking about prose rather than poetry here) be the priority. It sounds a very obvious point to make, but anyone who has to work at all with words (and that is almost all of us in our service economy) will know how easy it is to forget. Sometimes we ignore it because we are feeling lazy. Sometimes we avoid thinking through our meaning in a rigorous way because it means making tough judgements of our own – so we deliberately allow words to blur things a little at the edges. Sometimes, when we are working to a tight deadline, we simply do not have the time to pin our meaning down in a precise way, so we opt for words which will convey a general idea of what we are trying to say. I know I have been guilty of all these things, especially when, with a frowsty early-morning mind, I have been confronted with an especially complex story or one where there is a danger that I might get into trouble by betraying bias or expressing an un-politically correct idea.

But the fact that Orwell's principles are difficult to keep does not make them any less true, and they provide a kind of machete for fighting your way through the thickets of dilemmas you meet when you try to make your use of language PC. Do not refer to someone as 'differently abled' because the words do not match the meaning you are trying to convey. On the other hand, do not use the word 'businessmen' as a generic term for people in the business world because many of them are women. Say 'short' because we all know what that word means and it is a description, not a judgement – and so on. I am still not quite sure about 'chair', but there is obviously a perfectly respectable Orwellian case to be made that it is as foolish to call a woman a 'chairman' as it is to call her a piece of furniture. Even George Orwell would probably not have an answer to every question thrown up by living in a PC World, but he has a clear answer to that overwhelmingly important question, 'Who owns words?' None of us do: the only thing that really matters is their objective meaning.

George Orwell is something of a cult hero for people who work in my world. Bullshit-busting is, in an age of spin, what most of us aspire to be good at, and he did it better than anyone else. That and the fact that he could write in the sort of conversational tone that makes for really good broadcasting make him a natural role-model. But some specialists in linguistics are snooty about his ideas. The argument is that the Orwellian idea of language is flawed in its foundations because meaning, as one of them put it, 'is always on the slide'; time and context constantly change what a word denotes, and a word can never represent something in the precise way that, say, the figure 2 does. There is some truth in this. Take, for example, the description of St Paul's Cathedral, attributed to Charles II, as something 'awful, artificial and amusing'; in the seventeenth century this would have meant something that filled one with awe, displayed great artisanship and was pleasing to look upon. My grump about the confusing reversal of the word 'gay' above is another illustration of the point.

But Orwell's critics go beyond that. It is, they argue, naïve to assume that words can have a 'neutral' meaning – they always reflect cultural values. So when Orwell the essayist uses words, he cannot escape from Eric Blair the white English Old Etonian – and former colonial civil servant to boot. The meaning he attaches to them reflects that background, and it is dishonest to pretend he is in some way free from 'politics' in the way he writes. Orwell's language, so the argument runs, is every bit as politicised as that of the most radical feminist champion of She-gods and enemy of words like 'craftsmanship'. This argument, like the first objection to Orwell's theories, has some merit. If, for example, you are a former public schoolboy – as he was – your early understanding of the meaning of the word 'freedom' is likely to have been formed in the context of pettifogging school rules. But if you had grown up in a working-class family in the north-east at the time when Eric Blair was at Eton the concept of 'freedom' – or lack of it – probably had much more to do with what you could and could not do with the amount of money you had to spend. F.R. Leavis, the father of one of the most influential schools of English literary criticism and one of Orwell's near contemporaries, wrote, in *Education and the University* (published three years before 'Politics and the English Language'), that 'language is not a detachable instrument of thought and communication. It is the historical embodiment of its community's assumptions and aspirations at levels which are so subliminal much of the time that language is their only index.'

The problem with both the anti-Orwellian arguments is that if you follow them through to their natural conclusions you give up on the idea of meaning altogether. At least it is a problem for me, but not, apparently for those structuralists we met in the last chapter. I am indebted to Roger Kimball for this revealing passage – if you can bear to juggle so many interlocking authorial voices, Kimball is quoting a certain Professor Moxley on the subject of Jacques Derrida:

Derrida has shown that language is incapable of conveying the type of meaning that is usually ascribed to historical narratives. According to Derrida, linguistic signs are arbitrary constructs whose significance is impermanent and unstable. Language functions to suggest an absent presence of meaning. That is, the meanings of linguistic representations are always illusory, since they depend on metaphysical claims that cannot be substantiated.

So if you think everything you have so far read in this book is complete gibberish, neither of us need worry too much; all the tip-tapping away I have been doing on my laptop was simply designed to 'suggest an absent presence of meaning' anyway.

I abandoned mathematics when I was fifteen because I was asked to work out the gradient of a curve. This, of course, is impossible to do with total precision, because it is in the nature of a curve to change its gradient constantly. So we were taught a technique from what is known as calculus; it involved working out an approximation so near the non-existent truth that it could just as well serve as the answer to the question. But that was not good enough for me – I was full of that unforgiving certainty of the adolescent, a habit of mind probably made even more dangerous by a good dose of dogmatic Catholicism. The whole point of mathematics, I felt, was that it delivered certainty; ambiguity I could find aplenty in literature and the arts. I chucked in the idea of a maths

A level and focused on Latin; at least there you knew what the rules were.

Calculus, I now know, gave us Newton and Leibniz and modern physics. I was wrong, and have learnt to accept that you cannot always have absolute answers in science and mathematics. In just the same way, the fact that words can never denote things in the manner that, say, entries in a library catalogue can be directly matched to books on the shelves does not mean that we should lose sight of the fact that words matter first and foremost for their meaning. I am sure there is a technical philosophical term for the fallacy I am describing, but I would simply call it a counsel of despair. It is similar to the political argument that because we do not have the resources to intervene everywhere in the world where there is injustice we should not do so anywhere. F.R. Leavis, whom I have quoted above as an exponent of the idea that language is loaded with cultural assumptions, also gave us the concept of the 'third realm', something which is neither entirely subjective nor entirely objective; works of literature (and this could just as easily be applied to the meanings of words) 'which are not private like a dream or public in the sense of something that can be tripped over, but exist in human minds as a work of collaborative re-constitution'.

As soon as you think in practical terms you realise how important it is not to be seduced too completely by the cleverness of the idea that 'meaning is always on the slide'.

One of the best books I read while researching this one is called *The Morning After: Sex, Fear and Feminism.* The author, Katie Roiphe, finds herself caught up in what she feels to be near hysteria about rape on the American college campuses of the early 1990s. At her own university, Princeton, she attends a series of rallies held under the banner of the 'Take Back the Night movement', and as she listens to a procession of her contemporaries taking the microphone to describe their experiences of abuse she notes the following phenomenon:

The strange thing is that as these different girls – tall and short, fat and thin, nervous and confident – get up to give intensely personal accounts, all of their stories begin to sound the same. Listening to a string of them, I hear patterns begin to emerge. The same phrases float through different voices. Almost all of them begin 'I wasn't planning to speak out tonight but . . .', even the ones who had spoken out in previous years. They talk about feeling helpless, and feeling guilty. Some talk about hating their bodies. The echoes continue. 'I didn't admit or talk about it.' 'I was silenced.' 'I was powerless over my own body.' The catchwords travel across campuses, and across the boundaries between the spoken and written word.

The speakers are committing Orwell's cardinal sin of surrendering to the words; they are letting the approved language of the feminist orthodoxy of the day take over their own experiences. And the cost is to the true meaning of what they have been through. 'The individual power of each story,' Roiphe argues, 'is sapped by the collective mode of expression. The details fade, the stories blend together, sounding programmed and automatic . . . as intimate details are squeezed into formulaic standards, they tend to be wrought with an emotion more generic than heartfelt.' 'Orthodoxy, of whatever colour,' as Orwell put it, 'seems to demand a lifeless imitative style.'

Once the words take over, the very meaning of the word 'rape' is called into question; when the rhetoric of the movement takes flight and leaves meaning behind all forms of male seduction and persuasion can come to be seen as a form of rape. The founder of a rape prevention programme on one American campus complains that the seriousness of the crime is 'undermined by the growing tendency of some feminists to label all heterosexual miscommunication and insensitivity as acquaintance rape', and Roiphe adds, 'one woman, raped by a stranger at knife point, says that although she feels bad for women raped by their former boyfriend, she does not think their experience should be equated with hers'.

The other great value of the Orwellian principle of putting the meaning of a word before everything else is that it acts as a bulwark against the verbal bullies. I do not at all mind the fact that I now have to think quite carefully about the way I speak and write about issues like gender and race – in fact, I think my broadcasting is a great deal sharper and livelier precisely because I am constantly forced to question my own assumptions and prejudices in these areas. Self-criticism is a healthy habit, especially for those who work in an organisation like the BBC which has such a powerful public voice, and engaging in an intellectual exercise like the experiment I tried with 'nitty-gritty' at the beginning of this chapter can even be fun. I also completely accept that not bothering with these questions is not an option. The BBC acknowledges the political dimension of words all the time and tells us quite firmly what we should and should not say. The question of what we should call the barrier which the Israelis have built in the West Bank has, for example, been the subject of intense debate: the Israelis like to call it a 'security fence' because they claim it is there to keep out suicide bombers and 'fence' has less awkward connotations than 'wall'; the Palestinians say it is part of a land grab and call it a 'separation wall'. We just call it a barrier – not the most vivid word but most of us are happy to go along with it.

But I do very much resent being made to feel that if, after thinking hard about the balance between the Kudu Principle and Orwell's principle in a particular case, I favour one word or phrase over another, I have in some way shown myself to be insensitive or – worse – revealed some kind of inappropriate political bias. During the spate of murders of prostitutes in East Anglia in December 2006, for example, there was a case made that we should refer to the victims as 'sex workers' on the grounds that the word 'prostitute' is pejorative. It is perfectly true that 'prostitute' and 'prostitution' carry a weight of social dis-approval, but since that reflects the way most of us think about the practice I believe those are the right words to use; being a prostitute is not like working as a shop assist-ant or a banker, as most prostitutes (who have usually fallen into this way of earning money out of desperation) will tell you. I of course accept that others may take a different view – looking back at the cuttings during this period, for example, I notice that the *Guardian* goes for 'sex worker' – but I resent any suggestion that by calling someone a prostitute I am implying that I do not care what happens to them, which in the context of this particu-lar story would of course have been particularly callous.

Looking back over the last paragraph I realise I have committed a journalistic crime of which I am especially intolerant in others. Whenever anyone gives me a script which includes phrases like 'the case was made' or 'critics say' I demand to know a few basic facts. Who made this case? Who are these critics? What did they actually say? Off-the-shelf phrases like those usually mean something like 'this is a line we have chatted about at an editorial meeting and we thought we could work it up into a story' or 'a bloke in the pub said to me that . . .' And if I am honest, that is to some extent true in this case. We did have an interviewee on the programme arguing for the use of 'sex worker' rather than 'prostitute', but she did so perfectly politely and no one actually bullied me about sticking with the old-fashioned word or accused me of disregarding the fate of the victims. What then, I find myself asking, is the source of my resentment?

For an answer I am indebted to Deborah Cameron, the linguistics expert I have quoted earlier and who has written extensively on what she calls the 'Verbal Hygiene' movement. 'Meaning,' she writes, 'works by contrast; the words you choose acquire force from an implicit comparison with the ones you could have chosen, but did not.'

By coining alternatives to traditional usage, therefore, the radicals have effectively *politicised all the terms* [her italics]. They have made it impossible for anyone to speak or write without appearing to take up a political position, for which they can be held accountable. Thus if I say 'Ms X is the chair of Y' I convey one political standpoint; if I say 'Miss X is the chairman of Y' I convey another. What I cannot do any more is say either of these things and hope to convey by it only 'a certain woman holds a certain office in a certain organisation'.

It is this politicising of people's words against their will, rather than specific usages like 'African American' or 'physically challenged', that I believe many critics find deeply objectionable.

Reading this was something of a 'eureka' moment: that is precisely the source of my ill-defined resentment. Deborah Cameron's point is especially true for broadcasters and journalists. I feel especially grumpy when the task of writing an introduction for a guest on the *Today* programme – something which should take no more than a few moments – becomes a time-consuming and agonised process because of the kind of considerations she has in mind. X, whether she is a Miss or a Ms, a chairman or a chair, has been asked on to the programme because she has something important to say; that's where I want to focus my attention, and being *forced* to confront the PC dimension of a title feels like a needless obstacle. I need all my energies to identify what specifically matters about what she is saying now, not what my words mean in general terms about my view of women. Both things are of course important, but if she is – say – the head of a charity who wants to tell the world that large numbers of people are in imminent danger of starvation in a forgotten part of the globe, that matters much more than what I call her.

Deborah Cameron's insight provides the link between the vague sense of being bullied that I – and many others – have felt, and perhaps the most serious charge that is regularly made against the champions of PC: that they close down real debate on sensitive issues, and even try to limit free speech. Another of the authors I have quoted in the previous chapter, Stuart Hall, compared them to the Puritans of the seventeenth century; 'A strong strain of moral self-righteousness,' he writes, 'has often been PC's most characteristic "voice"'. That was written in the early 1990s, and fifteen years later the commentator Anthony Browne was writing in almost exactly the same terms in *The Retreat of Reason: Political Correctness and the Corruption of Public Debate in Modern Britain*: 'It is this self-righteous sense of virtue that makes the PC believe they are justified in suppressing freedom of speech,' he argued. 'Political correctness is the dictatorship of virtue.'

# 3

# Free speech in a PC World

I beseech you, in the bowels of Christ, think it possible
you may be mistaken.

Oliver Cromwell, *Letter to the*
*General Assembly of the Church of Scotland*


I interviewed the BBC's disability affairs correspondent,
Peter White, immediately after completing the last
chapter and found that I had developed the tiresome tic
of leaping on every parenthetical reference to PC language
like an over-enthusiastic puppy. 'Why?' I interrupted when
he mentioned, *en passant*, that he preferred the expression 'partially sighted' to 'visually impaired'. It was, he
explained, simply a matter of clarity – he feels that the
phrase 'visually impaired' is not likely to mean very much
to most people.

But Peter has little patience with the sort of word-
wormy agonising I have detailed in the previous chapter;
he is, for example, dismissive about the extensive debate
there has been over whether it is better to talk about

'people with disabilities' or 'disabled people'; the first is favoured by those who believe it is important to put the word 'people' before a reference to disability, the second by those of the Orwellian (in the sense that I have used the word in the last chapter) persuasion who value clarity. To Peter all of this is a distraction; his real quarrel with the notion of Political Correctness is that over-sensitivity about language can be actively damaging to real debate. 'I would never,' he said, 'pick you up on a phrase I didn't like – even if you talked about "the disabled", which makes it sound as if we have all been delivered in some vast pantechnicon.' He believes that if people are made to worry too much about the language they use it will stop them thinking clearly about things that matter – and, indeed, that we sometimes exploit the PC focus on appropriate language as an excuse for avoiding close discussion of issues that make us feel uncomfortable.

Take the debate over whether people with a low mental age should have sex. It is obviously an important one, and it raises moral questions which are both complex and intriguing, but it is not a subject most of us would enjoy discussing very much, particularly not in a public forum where others can pass judgement on our sensitivity (or lack of it); certainly I would not relish finding my name next to an item on the matter on a *Today* running order. The terms of the debate can be subtly shifted by the choice of words in which it is framed; for example, the idea of those with 'learning disabilities' having sex might seem easier to accept than the idea of those with a child-like understanding doing so. And if I were ever required to conduct a discussion of this kind on the air I can easily imagine focusing squeamishly on the appropriateness of various phrases as a way of keeping the real matter at stake at a safe distance.

Peter has been blind since birth, and he has especially strong views about the way discussion concerning the sort of education blind people should have is – in his judgement – being skewed by Political Correctness. When he was growing up it was considered natural to send boys and girls like him to special boarding schools from a very early age – he went at five, a tough challenge for any child and, one would imagine, especially so for one suffering from the isolation of blindness. The modern orthodoxy is that blind children should be 'included' in mainstream schools, and the very word for this policy, the cuddly sounding 'inclusion', makes it difficult to disagree with. Peter does not, in fact, disagree with the general principle behind the inclusive philosophy, but he does think that there are sometimes pragmatic reasons for at least considering the specialist alternative. He pointed out, by way of illustration, that Braille needs to be learnt at a very young age if a blind person is going to use it with the fluency he finds he needs for his own job as a broadcaster, and he said that was much more easily achieved in the sort of special school he attended.

He also cited a story he was then covering about a

teenage boy who was going progressively blind. 'Everyone who cares about him,' he said, 'can see that it would be best for him to go to a special school, and he wants that too. But the local authority insist he can be provided for in the ordinary school he is attending.' Politically correct orthodoxy, he said, was being given priority over a pragmatic assessment of what was best in an individual case. Listening to him describe his dealings with a well-intentioned but obstinate local authority official over the case helped to crystallise my sense of one of the raw edges of the PC culture that makes so many of us feel uneasy. There is no Great Book that stands to PC-ism as, say, *Das Kapital* stands to Communism; but it does have the characteristics of at least a close cousin of the Stalinist and Maoist concept of 'Correct Line-ism', the conviction that an orthodoxy, once agreed upon, must never be questioned.

The suspicion that PC inhibitions might be stifling debate has been worrying away at the edge of my consciousness since a talk I gave in the summer of 2004 to the Churches Media Council, a group which brings together Christian leaders, journalists and broadcasters for an annual think-fest about the state of religious broadcasting. My subject was the way Islam is represented on the air, and I managed to shock some of my audience rather more than I had intended. Many of you will no doubt be familiar with the conceit of the H.M. Bateman cartoons known as 'The Man Who ...' series; published in the *Tatler* just before the First World War, they sent up various forms of British stuffiness by depicting bufferish characters – with exploding red faces and flying facial hair – reacting in horror to such social catastrophes as 'The Man Who Ate His Luncheon in the Royal Enclosure', and 'The Man Who Passed the Port the Wrong Way'. By the time I sat down after the 'q and a' at the Churches Media Council I knew what it must have felt like to be that Ascot race-goer tucking into his sandwiches while grown men in morning coats crashed to the floor in horror all around him.

I had just completed recording a four-part series for Radio Four called *In the Footsteps of Mohammed*, and in the previous couple of months I had been forced to confront the depths of my own ignorance about Islam. I had learnt about the way Muslim scholars translated classical Greek texts into Arabic, preserving them for later generations of Christian thinkers. I had admired the gorgeousness of buildings like the Alhambra and the Great Mosque of Cordoba – evidence of an extraordinarily cultivated European Muslim civilisation which had, as far as I can remember, almost entirely escaped my attention during all those years I spent studying literature and history at school and university. And in Indonesia, the world's most populous Muslim country, I had spoken to politicians and thinkers engaged in the great enterprise of trying to reconcile traditional Islamic teaching and modern ideas about pluralism and democracy.

I had also done my best to get a sense of the true meaning of the concept of *jihad*, reading the appropriate passages of the Koran and interviewing Muslim experts in the field.

I consider myself reasonably literate in religious terms, so it was a shock to find that so much of the material we covered in the series came as news to me; it made me reflect on the way we treat Islam as broadcasters and journalists, and I decided to use my invitation to the conference to play some clips of the kind of material about Islam you do not usually hear on the airwaves. I played, for example, part of an interview I had conducted with a highly articulate Saudi woman who had earned a reputation as a kind of Islamic Anne Atkins – the sort of figure who would have been selected to do the Saudi version of *Thought for the Day* if such a thing were ever to be created. She spoke passionately about her personal relationship with the Prophet Mohammed in very much the way some Christians speak about a personal relationship with Jesus. It was a moving performance, and I used it to make the point that we very seldom hear Muslims talking in purely spiritual – as opposed to political or social – terms about their faith.

I also played them an extract from an interview with Dr Azzam Tamimi, director of a London-based body called the Institute of Islamic Political Thought; it was set up to encourage new ideas in Islam and to explore ways of making the religion relevant to modern political issues, and Dr Tamimi seemed just the man to unravel the complex idea of *jihad* in a way that was both scholarly and accessible to a Radio Four audience. He began promisingly enough:

[During] the first thirteen years of Islam, the word *jihad* was mentioned in the early Koranic revelation to demand of Muslims to restrain themselves and not respond to violence with violence. So *jihad* for the first thirteen years was about restraining yourself and not using violence. Now when the Muslim community was banished from their home town in Mecca, were thrown out or forced out, they sought refuge in another town – Medina – and they formed with the host community a state of their own. That state became so vulnerable and under threat and they needed to defend themselves. And this is when the Koran clearly states that now you are permitted to fight and do the things you were forbidden from before. So first it was forbidden, then it became permitted, and then at a later stage it became compulsory. When you are attacked, it becomes compulsory – incumbent upon you – to fight back. And this is what many people do not appreciate about what's going on in the Muslim lands today for instance. The Palestinians who are fighting occupation are simply called terrorists. From an Islamic perspective, they're doing the right thing. They're doing the noble thing, because you shouldn't allow an invader to take your land and rob you of your resources.

*Question (slightly verbose) from ES*: You mentioned the Palestinians as an illustration of the way the concept is misunderstood often, from the outside. Is there anything that lays down what can or cannot be done in defence of your country if you feel it's being invaded? The obvious point of that question being, of course, suicide bombers, and whether *jihad* and the duties laid on you by *jihad* justify that particular form of violence.

*Answer*: There is an elaborate code of conduct for the battlefield that Muslims are supposed to adhere to. And the best manifestation of this is the sermon given by the first caliph to succeed the Prophet in governance when he bade farewell to the army going to northern Arabia to fight the Byzantine troops. He said to them, 'Remember that you are proceeding for the sake of God, so always have piety and fear God. Do not fight those who do not fight you. Do not kill women and children. You will be coming across people who have secluded themselves in monasteries and places of worship. Leave them alone and do not approach them. Do not destroy crops, do not burn trees, do not, do not, do not, etc. . . .' Something more elaborate than the Geneva Convention I would say. However, in history, as well as in contemporary times, there are always exceptions to the rule, as always. If you're fighting a conventional warfare and there is a defined battlefield, you have to adhere to these values. But if you are invaded by an enemy, and that enemy takes your land and takes your home and throws you out, and no one is coming to your help, and the enemy is not willing to listen – then . . . you are permitted to devise and innovate methods of fighting back until the enemy recognises your rights. And the human bomb in Palestine comes within this context.

Q: It does, in, in, in your judgement, that is justified . . .
A: That's the . . .
Q: . . . and within the r . . .
A: . . . judgement . . .
Q: That's within the rules?
A: That's the judgement of the overwhelming majority of Muslim scholars . . .

The difficulty the transcriber had in capturing the final part of the exchange accurately reflects my confusion; the sort of civilised academic we turn to for expert advice on Radio Four is not supposed to turn from Jekyll to Hyde in the middle of the interview, suddenly revealing himself to be a fanatic who believes that it is a religious duty to blow yourself up, killing innocent men, women and children in the process. The man had turned up at the studio wearing a jacket and tie, for goodness sake!

The point at which I played the extract to the Churches Media Council was the point at which I began to feel that I was 'The Man Who Said "Bum" at the Vicarage Tea Party'. The interview was shocking not just because of the support Dr Tamimi gave to suicide bombing, but because – critically – of the way that view was placed in the context of Islamic history and contemporary thinking: 'this,' he was saying, 'is the mainstream scholarly view.'

There are, of course, many people who would challenge that, but I had talked to enough Muslim thinkers in the course of making my series on Islam to conclude that Dr Tamimi was far from being alone. And yet his views were ones we very, very seldom heard expressed on mainstream television and radio programmes – certainly not at the time I recorded the programmes. Was that, I found myself asking, because of Political Correctness? Had we been too ready to accept the PC orthodoxy about the way Islam should be covered – and had that led us to suppress discussion of aspects of the religion we found it awkward to confront? Had we, in fact, been guilty of self-censorship?

Open, formal censorship can be surprisingly easy to deal with; you know what the rules are and you can try to plan your way around them if you want to. When I worked in Baghdad as a reporter for ITN during the first Gulf War we had to operate through a formal military and political censorship regime – all my reports were watched by a 'minder' from Saddam's regime – and we developed a little game to mitigate the impact. There was an anti-aircraft emplacement just outside the hotel window, and the Iraqis insisted that its location was a military secret (since it fired at coalition planes bombing Baghdad on almost every night of the week I was never quite sure of the logic of this, but no matter). We knew that if we included any shots of the guns in our report the minder would make us take them out – so sometimes we put the pictures in quite deliberately, in the hope that it would distract his attention from a more subtle point I was trying to make elsewhere in the piece. Usually, it worked. Dealing with the subtler forms of censorship that sometimes arise in pluralistic and open societies like our own can be much more difficult – not least because very often one does not recognise them for what they are.

In 1986 – during my first year as Washington correspondent for Channel 4 News – I was despatched to cover a story in rural Tennessee, and as my camera crew and I drove deeper into ever thicker pine forests I was reminded that rural America really is remote from modern urban life in a way you simply no longer find in Britain. The trees closed around us and the homesteads – many of them flying the Confederate flag – grew smaller and scruffier; I had a sense of entering an older, unreformed America of hillbillies and dark, secret deeds. Most stories I covered as a Washington correspondent in those days fell into one of two categories, and both reflected the Euro-centric view of my news desk in London: to get on the air a story either had to touch on the Cold War and the possibility of imminent nuclear conflagration – a perfectly understandable European preoccupation – or it had to speak to the overwhelmingly prevalent prejudice back home that all Americans were, in the last analysis, completely bonkers. The story I was on my way to cover quite definitely fell into the second category. A Federal Appeals Court was due to rule on *Mozert v.*

*Hawkins County Board of Education*, a long-running legal challenge which a group of Tennessee parents had brought against their local education authority. They were Christian fundamentalists, and they charged that their children were being corrupted by the texts the local school board had authorised for reading classes; *Goldilocks and the Three Bears*, it was for example alleged, was an improper story because it failed to show the heroine receiving the appropriate punishment for breaking and entering and stealing someone else's porridge.

One of the schools at the centre of the row kindly agreed to allow us to film in a classroom of eight-year-olds, and the teacher introduced us at the start of their lesson by explaining that 'this camera crew comes from England'. This remark was greeted by looks of blank incomprehension, and she hastily added, 'Oh, I guess we didn't get to England yet.' I had been living in the United States for some six months by this stage, and had just begun to fall in love with the beguiling life it is possible to enjoy there; I have to admit my new infatuation was somewhat shaken by this trip. The parents bringing the case were from central casting – the language they spoke was recognisably English, but their views were so far from anything I had ever heard before that they might as well have been speaking an alien tongue from some far-flung galaxy. The office in London, of course, loved the piece. In due course the parents were defeated by a ruling from the Supreme Court, and I put the whole thing

down as one of those amusing but ultimately inconse-
quential pieces of Americana that make the life of a
Washington correspondent such fun.

I was wrong: the case did in fact have very serious
implications for freedom of speech in the United States,
and I shall explain why in a moment or two. The reason
I missed the importance of the story was, I now think,
that, still new to the American experience as I was, the
incredibly robust journalistic climate in the Washington
of those days had fooled me about attitudes to free
speech in the United States. In the mid 1980s the
culture of the American press generally and the White
House press corps in particular was intrusive and aggres-
sive. Coming from the still deferential world of the
British journalism of the time, I was constantly struck
by the confidence of my American colleagues; their
assumption that they had a 'right to know' anything they
wanted was, it seemed, ironclad. Perhaps the best
known exponent of the American broadcasting style
then was Sam Donaldson, the White House correspondent of ABC News. Donaldson had a voice like a bull-
horn and would persecute President Reagan with
shouted questions at every conceivable opportunity.
Reagan dubbed him – in most un-PC language that a
president would certainly not use today – 'the Ayatollah
of the press corps'. In his autobiography Donaldson
summed up his journalistic philosophy like this:

If you send me to cover a pie-baking contest on Mother's Day, I'm going to ask dear old Mom whether she used artificial sweetener in violation of the rules, and while she's at it, could I see the receipt for the apples to prove she didn't steal them. I maintain that if Mom has nothing to hide, no harm will have been done. The questions should be asked. Too often, Mom, and presidents – behind those sweet faces – turn out to have stuffed a few rotten apples in the public barrel.

So when I cover a president, I try to remember two things: first, if you don't ask, you don't find out; and, second, the questions don't do the damage. Only the answers do.

As a very, very junior member of the White House press corps, I used to stand at the back during presidential photo-calls and watch in awe as Donaldson bawled his fearlessly blunt interrogations at the most powerful man in the world. Truly, I thought, this is the land of the free.

But while researching this book I discovered that the story I covered in Tennessee all those years ago did not have quite such a happy ending. Educational publishers are businesses, not crusaders, and although the publishers of the Holt Family Readers (the textbooks at the centre of the case) won in court, they paid a heavy price in commercial terms. According to one account of the incident, the Holt Readers, 'once the most popular series in the nation', were 'brought to the verge of extinction' by the episode. What responsible educational authority would turn to books which had stirred up such controversy, after all? 'If publishers learnt a lesson from the saga of the Holt reading series,' wrote Diane Ravitch, a prominent educational historian, 'it was the importance of avoiding controversy by censoring themselves in advance and including nothing that might attract bad publicity or litigation.'

The story is told in Diane Ravitch's book *The Language Police*, perhaps the best book about freedom of speech in a PC World I have read. Published in 2003, it presents a genuinely frightening picture of a semi-secret web of self-censorship in the United States.

One of the reasons it is so powerful is that it draws on the author's own experience. President Clinton invited her to join an educational board charged with the design of a new national testing system, and when she and her fellow board members drew up what they thought was an appropriate selection of passages to test reading skills they encountered a previously unknown – to me anyway – academic species called the 'bias and sensitivity reviewers'. The job of these panels – they are, it turns out, a well-established presence in the American educational establishment – is to sniff out anything that could disadvantage or distract any particular group of children taking a test in the American schools system. The objections they had to some of the passages chosen by Diane Ravitch and her colleagues are truly startling. It is worth quoting a couple of them in full:

THE BLIND MOUNTAIN CLIMBER. One of the stranger recommendations of the bias and sensitivity panel involved a true story about a heroic young blind man who hiked to the top of Mount McKinley; the highest peak in North America. The story described the dangers of hiking up an icy mountain trail, especially for a blind person. The panel voted 12–11 to eliminate this inspiring story. First, the majority maintained that the story contained 'regional bias' because it was about hiking and mountain climbing, which favours students who live in regions where those activities are common. Second, they rejected the passage because it suggested that people who are blind are at a disadvantage compared to people who have normal sight, that they are 'worse off' and have a more difficult time facing dangers than those who are not blind . . . CLASS DISTINCTIONS IN THE ANCIENT WORLD. The bias panel did not like a story about growing up in ancient Egypt. The story contrasted how people's ways of living varied in accordance with their wealth and status. Some lived in palaces, others were noblemen, others were farmers and city workers. The size and grandeur of one's house, said the story, depended on family wealth. To the naked eye, the story was descriptive, not judgemental. But the bias and sensitivity reviewers preferred to eliminate it, claiming that references to wealth and class distinctions had an 'elitist' tone . . .

And so – eccentrically – it goes on. Aesop's fable of 'The Fox and the Crow' is out on the grounds of gender bias (the vain and foolish crow who is flattered into singing so that she opens her beak and drops her lump of cheese for the fox below is, of course, female, and the clever, flattering fox is male), and out too goes the history of Mount Rushmore, the giant carving of some of the United States' greatest presidents in South Dakota, on the grounds that it is an 'abomination' to some Native Americans.

Inspired by this experience, Ravitch embarked on a wide-ranging investigation of the phenomenon of bias and sensitivity reviewing, and her book piles up the evidence about the impact of what is apparently standard practice in the world of school testing and academic publishing in the United States. Her appendix of 'Words, Usages, Stereotypes, and Topics' which are banned by the codes of named academic publishers runs to some fifteen pages, from 'Able-bodied (banned as offensive, replace with *person who is non-disabled*)' through 'Hussy (banned as sexist)' and 'Huts (banned as ethnocentric, replace with *small houses*)', on to 'Polo (banned as elitist)' and 'Regatta (banned as elitist)', 'Waitress (banned as sexist, replace with *server*, *waitron*) and 'White (banned as adjective meaning pure)', ending, in a double-whammy flourish of anti-elitism and anti-sexism, with 'Yacht' and 'Yes-man'. Diane Ravitch has added pages and pages of images and topics to be avoided too ('African Americans as Physically Powerful' and, bizarrely, 'Blizzards' among them). There is something about gathering banned words or ideas into a list which makes the absurdity of censorship especially apparent – any compilation of this kind is bound to remind one of the infamous 'Index' of books which were forbidden to the Catholic faithful right up until the 1960s.

There is no one forcing these publishers and test-setters to proscribe great swathes of the English language and its literature; they are doing it, Diane Ravitch argues, partly out of an admirable desire to be sensitive to the needs of students (like my BBC colleague Peter White, she believes that well-intentioned people with the best of motives are often responsible for the worst excesses of Political Correctness) and partly by the commercially sensible desire to avoid the sort of controversy that got the Holt Readers into such trouble. But the result is, as she puts it, a 'regime of censorship that has quietly spread through educational publishing'. On the basis of the evidence she has assembled, it is difficult to disagree with that conclusion, and discreet self-censorship on a huge scale is, in its way, every bit as corrosive as overt, straightforward censorship imposed from above by government fiat.

There is, of course, PC form here; one of the things that so enraged the Right during the academic debates of the 1980s I have described in Chapter 1 were the so-called 'Speech Codes' introduced by American universities. The codes regulated the sort of language students could use in a way designed to prevent minority groups being insulted or suffering discrimination – again, a perfectly

worthy objective, but some of the more extreme examples of Political Correctness thrown up in the process
made easy targets for satire. One university administrator
in California campaigned against the phrases 'a nip in the
air' and a 'chink in one's armour' ('How about banning
fruit-tree as disparaging to homosexuals?' demanded one
enraged critic). And the codes were widely attacked
because of the punitive way in which they were enforced.
Nat Hentoff, a writer who became perhaps the most
dogged chronicler of code-ist outrages, cited another
example from California, where a campus code banned
what were described as 'fighting words'. 'These are the
kinds of words that are "inherently likely to provoke
violent reaction, *whether or not they actually do*"'
(emphasis added by Hentoff). And the penalty for
violating the code could be very serious indeed: 'he or
she who fires a fighting word at any ordinary person,'
Hentoff reported, 'can be reprimanded or dismissed from
the university because the perpetrator should "reasonably know" that what he or she has said will interfere
with the "victim's ability to pursue effectively his or her
education or otherwise participate fully in the university
programs and activities".' Hentoff was also able to report
that at the great University of Stanford, no less, a student
leader gave a speech arguing that 'We don't put enough
restrictions on freedom of speech.'

But this sort of thing was not, of course, the preserve
of PC-ers. The Tennessee parents I met, for example,

would have been horrified to have heard themselves described in that way. And Diane Ravitch – although she can be broadly described as a right-wing intellectual – is scrupulously even-handed in the way she picks up on the censoring idiocies of the Right as well those of the Left. She recalls her own youth in Texas when a crusading member of the Houston school board fought tirelessly – and successfully – to ban economics and geography books which contained any positive reference to the United Nations and its 'one world government' philosophy. She details the various Christian fundamentalist campaigns to purge textbooks of references to abortion, divorce and homosexuality, and to exclude reading material that dabbled in magic, fantasy, witches and the like, even if it was drawn from classic works of children's literature like C.S. Lewis's Narnia stories, which owe so much to the Christian tradition. The Australian cultural critic Robert Hughes, looking at America with the eyes of an outsider, coined a new phrase to describe this variety of right-wing, Christian fundamentalist PC: he called it Patriotic Correctness.

It is a very good phrase for describing what has happened to public debate in the United States since the Al Qaeda attacks of 11 September 2001. George W. Bush's America has at times seemed like a country where the Sam Donaldsons who asked the difficult questions have been silenced. I make this judgement somewhat tentatively – since I do not spend nearly as much time in the

United States as I used to – but when I watch American television news programmes now the admirably cantankerous spirit I remember with such awe and affection seems to have disappeared. That is partly a reflection of the soul-searching that has afflicted the American media since the Reagan/Donaldson years; its role in the Monica Lewinsky affair and the attempt to impeach Bill Clinton, for example, led many journalists and broadcasters to question whether they really did have a 'right to know' and publish absolutely everything. But it is also, surely, a reflection of the Patriotic Correctness that has gripped so much of America since President Bush declared his war on terror.

I was lucky enough to find myself on Capitol Hill with a microphone on the night of the address President Bush made to the joint houses of Congress in the immediate aftermath of the dreadful events of 11 September 2001. It was a bravura performance; Tony Blair and his entourage dined at the White House that night and his communications director, Alastair Campbell, later told me that the British party had all been struck by the extraordinarily calm confidence Bush displayed before making the speech. And it was exactly the kind of speech a traumatised American people needed that night: fighting talk, telling them that there was a way to strike back.

But the speech was based on a starkly Manichean view of the world: there was, the President seemed to be saying, a long war to be fought between the forces of

good and the forces of evil. Everyone – every government, he made explicitly clear – must choose which side
they backed, and expect to be treated accordingly. There
was no room in this world view for the middle ground –
or for shades of grey in the analysis. When he sat down
to a thunderous ovation, two huge and related questions
remained unasked: what ideology could possibly have
driven the men who undertook such desperate acts, and
why do some people in the world hate the United States?
Understanding why someone commits a terrible wrong
is not the same as accepting that it has some justification
– it is simply a wise thing to try to do when you are facing
a challenge from a powerful adversary. But the strong
primary colours in which George Bush painted events
that night excluded any possibility of subtler questions
about the motives of the terrorists. They were evil, and
that was that – to reflect any further on the matter was,
it seemed, not Patriotically Correct.

After the speech I interviewed Senator John Warner
– famous mostly for having once been married to
Elizabeth Taylor, but also, more recently and interest-
ingly, for emerging as one of the Republican critics of
the White House policy in Iraq – and he told me that
it was the greatest speech ever made by an American
president. What about the Gettysburg Address, the FDR
and JFK inaugurals, I found myself wondering. But to
the extent that the President's speech established a tone
of public debate that would endure, the senator was on

to something. George Bush caught and defined a public mood that night. It was to sustain his presidency through to a second term, and it gave him a degree of immunity from criticism over some civil liberties questions – like those raised by Guantanamo Bay – which would have boiled the steam out of Sam Donaldson's ears in the Reagan days.

Somewhere in the American soul there is a twitch towards censorship. I missed it when I was based there because I was intoxicated by the excitement of working in such a noisy and robust journalistic culture, so refreshing after the fustiness of mid-1980s Britain. But it is there. Because of the free speech guarantees of the First Amendment we tend to think of the United States as a country where the commitment to freedom of expression is absolute and beyond question – and I found that my own experience of working there reinforced that view. But it is in fact a country where authoritarian and libertarian instincts are constantly at war with one another (think, after all, of Prohibition and McCarthyism); that is one of the reasons why Political Correctness took root in the United States so much earlier than it did here.

In Britain our PC battles are generally fought on a more modest scale. While I was working on this book I received an email from the columnist Mary Kenny:

Look forward to the book [she wrote]. I know a lot of PC is a well-meaning effort to reintroduce manners and morals, and much of it not dissimilar to what I was taught in my Irish convent school in the late 1950s (do not use unkind words about people's disabilities, put yourself in the place of others, do not use rude words about people's origins, etc., etc.). The *Today* programme (and the *Moral Maze*) are indeed rare havens of more independence, but one couldn't say the same for a lot of the programming ... Radio 4 is a stage army of perfectly nice, well-educated folk all of whom share the same values. That's the real problem with PC – it's not that it's bad: it's that it's stiflingly conformist and does not allow for more challenging or counter-cultural attitudes. I would have made the same criticism of my convent education. I hope you will be able to represent that point. I'll stop now, I promise!

While America's intellectuals go head to head about Big Questions like academic freedom and the tone of political discourse, we worry about the soul of Radio Four (and, as one of its employees, I of course applaud the recognition of the network's importance that implies). But the idea that what hits America first eventually hits us too does seem to hold good in this instance, and there has recently been a slew of books on this side of the Atlantic taking up the anti-PC cudgels. Many of them have been more squibbish than the weighty volumes about higher education which deluged the American market fifteen to twenty years ago. James Delingpole's *How to be Right* asks, 'ARE YOU SICK AND TIRED OF BEING POLITICALLY CORRECT? TOO SCARED TO SPEAK

FOR FEAR OF BEING CALLED A FASCIST?' If your answer to those questions is yes you can enjoy the author's un-PC views on an alphabetical list of topics such as the EU, Germans and, of course, BBC bias. *Littlejohn's Britain* – which hit the top of the *Sunday Times* bestseller list in 2007 – took similar aim at the developments during the Blair years that the professionally irascible eponymous author particularly dislikes.

The 2007 pamphlet I quoted in Chapter 1, Anthony Browne's *The Retreat of Reason: Political Correctness and the Corruption of Public Debate in Modern Britain* is a more cerebral offering – it has footnotes, opens with quotations from Thomas Jefferson and Sidney Hook, and was published as a pamphlet by the think-tank Civitas. Its principal subject is that of this chapter; Browne's case is that in Britain today 'Members of the public, academics, journalists and politicians are afraid of thinking certain thoughts. People are vilified if they publicly diverge from accepted beliefs, sacked or even investigated by police for crimes against received wisdom. Whole areas of debate have been closed down by the crushing dominance of the moralistic ideology of political correctness.'

I feel a sort of spurious responsibility for some of the attention the book attracted because when it came out I held the ring (or tried to) during an extraordinarily ill-tempered exchange between the columnist Yasmin Alibhai-Brown and the author on the *Today* programme;

Anthony Browne says in a postscript to the second edition that their row 'had TV links vehicles and radio cars queuing up outside my flat'. Usually when two adversaries meet in the programme Green Room before or after coming on the air, they manage to be personally pleasant to one another – in fact the atmosphere in there is often quite jolly. Not on this occasion. Browne wrote, 'Both before and after the show, my flagellator refused to speak to me other than to snap that I was hysterical and poisonous.' Alibhai-Brown took her swipe in a subsequent column in the *Independent*: she said that Browne 'freely fabricates, accuses and insinuates throughout this shabby pamphlet'.

Browne has some striking examples of areas where he argues that open debate has been suppressed by PC anxieties, and he can turn a phrase nicely in a way that brings the constellation of issues that swirl around the phrase 'Political Correctness' sharply into focus. I quoted earlier his view that it is a 'self-righteous sense of virtue that makes the PC believe they are justified in suppressing freedom of speech. Political correctness is the dictatorship of virtue.' I think the idea that there is a strong strain of Puritanism in Political Correctness is a fruitful one, and I shall be developing it in Chapter 5. However, I did have, as they say, 'a problem' with Browne's pamphlet; on almost every occasion when he wrote about a story or topic I knew from direct personal experience, his allegations were factually inaccurate.

He stated, for example, that 'Migrationwatch, founded by former ambassador Sir Andrew Green, a lone group campaigning for less immigration against literally dozens of groups promoting mass immigration ... is almost totally blackballed by the BBC'; I have interviewed Sir Andrew Green on *Today* on many occasions. He claims that during the election campaigns in Iraq in 2005 'the politically correct left – including the *Guardian*, the *Independent* and most of the BBC' supported the suicide bombers and failed to celebrate the bravery of ordinary Iraqis because the elections were sponsored by the United States; I was in Baghdad for the election of January 2005 and we repeatedly stressed the bravery of people who went in such large numbers to the polls – not for any ideological reasons, but because it was so obviously the big story of those elections. He states that 'the BBC repeats everything that Liberty [the civil rights group] says with such unquestioning respect that they treat it often as a justification for a story in itself, with no counter-balancing points of view, even though Liberty is tied closely to the Labour party and cannot be described as politically neutral'; on almost every occasion when I have interviewed Liberty's director, Shami Chakrabarti, she has been attacking the Labour government over some aspect or other of its anti-terrorism legislation. During the Conservative Party Conference of 2007 the *Daily Telegraph* included her in its list of 'Big Hitters who shape thinking and policy on the Right', and when I mentioned

Browne's comment to her at a drinks party she nearly choked on her finger food.

All of these inaccuracies arise from the way Browne uses the evidence to make his point, and it does rather undermine his claim that Political Correctness distorts reality for ideological reasons: 'In the topsy turvy world of political correctness,' he writes, 'truth comes in two forms: the factually correct and the politically correct. The politically correct truth is publicly proclaimed correct by politicians, celebrities and the BBC even if it is wrong, while factually correct truth is publicly condemned as wrong even when it is right.' One of the peculiarities of this whole debate is the way almost everyone involved commits the sins of which they accuse their opponents.

There is a deeper mistake behind Browne's tendency to ideologically driven inaccuracy; it is one that echoes what is wrong with the more extreme American writing I have quoted and also explains some of the confusion and ill feeling generated by this subject in both countries. Brown writes about Political Correctness as if it is a coherent belief system, like Marxism or Catholicism. The formal definition he offers of the phenomenon is 'an ideology that classifies certain groups of people as victims in need of protection from criticism, and which makes believers feel that no dissent should be tolerated'. It may sometimes do both those things, but if I have learnt anything in the course of researching this book it is that PC means so many different things to different people and springs from such varied motives that it cannot make sense to call it 'an ideology'. It may sometimes reflect an ideology, but that is a different thing. If, for example, you are a passionate campaigner for gay rights or for feminism, you might espouse certain attitudes which others regard as PC, but your ideology would be gay rights or feminism. It is unlikely that you would describe yourself as a Political Correctness campaigner or a PC-ist.

Once you have made the mistake of thinking of Political Correctness as an ideology you can write about it in the sort of sweeping terms you might legitimately have used about, say, Communism. In Chapter 1 I have quoted a passage from Browne's vision of a world dominated by PC ideas, and there is plenty more in the chapter entitled 'The Triumph of Political Correctness'. We read that in twenty-first-century Britain

Political correctness has gained power over public services, from schools and hospitals to local authorities and central government. Political correctness became institutionalised at the BBC, but also started exerting control over ITV and the broadsheet newspapers. Politically correct alternative comedians quickly swept to power, becoming the new establishment, while PC triumphed in the literary field. PC triumphed not just in trade unions and charities, but in professional and trade associations, from medical Royal Colleges to business associations. Finally, even multinationals and the police started succumbing to PC.

He describes it as 'the national ideology' and even writes of its 'methodology'. Later in the book he refers to 'the oligarchs of political correctors'. All this sounds very impressive – and scary – but I am not sure what it actually means. 'Institutionalised' Political Correctness sounds suspiciously like 'institutional racism', a concept which I imagine Anthony Browne would regard as dubious in the extreme. And these generalisations tell us much, much less about Political Correctness than the acute observations of someone like Peter White, who has long practical experience in a particular field – or, come to that, than some of Anthony Browne's own concrete examples of debates that have been distorted by politically correct considerations.

I confess that I felt I was getting lost in the fog of war at this point. People I respected – those I interviewed formally, like Peter White, but also many others to whom I talked informally about this book – had told me they were worried that Political Correctness was stifling debate, and the same worry had been nagging away at me for several years. Some of the material I had read contained compelling evidence of concrete cases of censorship. And yet even serious attempts to get to the heart of the problem (and Anthony Browne's book is certainly that) seemed full of inconsistencies. The symptoms of the unease so many of us have felt about Political Correctness were easy enough to diagnose, but the disease itself – particularly the British strain – seemed impossible to identify with clarity.

Help came in the briefest of conversations with the Chief Rabbi, Sir Jonathan Sacks, who, in a snatched moment before delivering one of his *Thought for the Day* scripts, suggested I read two of the classic English texts on freedom of speech, Milton's *Areopagitica* and John Stuart Mill's *On Liberty*.

Milton's piece took its name from the Athenian hill where the highest judicial tribunal of the world's first democracy used to meet, and was written in the form of a *Speech . . . for the liberty of Unlicensed Printing to the Parliament of England*, Parliament having recently passed an Order which required that only material which had been approved and licensed should be printed. It was published in 1644 and never actually delivered as a speech, which was probably just as well since it is extremely long and some passages are so convoluted by Milton's love of a Latinate style that you need to read them two or three times before you understand what the great man is driving at. Milton plays heavily on the anti-Catholic prejudices of his intended audience, reminding them that the Roman Church routinely censored with 'those catalogues and expurging indexes that rake through the entrails of many an old good author with a violation worse than any could be offered to his tomb'. With the recent debate about religious hatred in mind, it is jolly to read Milton's description of the Catholic practice of insisting that all written material must be given an official *Imprimatur* (the word means 'let it be printed'): 'their last invention,' he writes, 'was to ordain that no book, pamphlet, or paper should be printed (as if St Peter had bequeathed them the keys of the press also out of Paradise) unless it were approved and licensed under the hands of two or three glutton friars.' Talk about stereotyping!

Milton also plays the patriotic card very well, telling his audience that they governed 'a nation not slow and dull, but of a quick, ingenious and piercing spirit, acute to invent, subtle and sinewy to discourse', and later, 'a mansion-house of Liberty'. It is difficult today not to smile at his suggestion that 'God is decreeing to begin some new and great period in his church, even to reforming the reformation itself; what does he then but reveal himself to his servants, and, as his manner is, first to his Englishmen?' But we need to remember that the *Areopagitica* was written in the middle of the English Civil War, when both sides felt they were caught up in a great existential struggle, and even after the three and a half centuries that have elapsed since its publication, it is moving to read Milton's famous vision of a new England being born in liberty as

a noble and puissant nation rousing itself like a strong man after sleep, and shaking her invincible locks; methinks I see her as an eagle mewing her mighty youth, and kindling her undazzled eyes at the full midday beam, purging and unscaling her long-abused sight at the fountain itself of heavenly radiance, while the whole noise of timorous and flocking birds, with those also that love the twilight, flutter about amazed at what she means, and in their envious gabble would prognosticate a year of sects and schisms.

Milton is relevant to today's debate about Political Correctness because he was part of a movement that shared some of the characteristics of the modern phenomenon. He was broadly on the same side as the censoring parliamentarians he addressed in the *Areopagitica*, and even in this thunderous plea for the importance of free thought and speech you are constantly reminded of the tension between his libertarian instincts and his conviction that he and those who thought like him were RC – by which, of course, I mean 'religiously correct' rather than Roman Catholic.

And yet he built his case around two thoroughly un-PC ideas. The first was that truth can stand up for itself without needing special protection: 'And though all the winds of doctrine were let loose to play upon the earth,' he writes, 'so truth be in the field, we do injuriously by licensing and prohibiting her strength. Let her and falsehood grapple; who ever knew truth put to the worse in a free and open encounter?' I have often thought of that principle when listening to some of my fellow Catholics and Christians complaining about the way our faith is attacked and ridiculed in the media. I went to see *Jerry Springer the Opera*, the satirical musical which provoked so much protest from Christian groups when it was broadcast on the BBC, and when I heard Jesus sing to the devil, 'You didn't give a toss, when I was hanging on the cross,' I found myself physically shivering because of the way the rhyme brought those two powerful words into such close juxtaposition. It was certainly blasphemous – in a very deliberate way. But it was also very, very funny, and thought-provoking, and I strongly believe that a faith which cannot survive laughter is not worth holding.

Milton's second insight was the hugely revolutionary idea that truth is divisible. It must have required a extra-ordinary effort of imagination to grasp the implications of that in seventeenth-century Europe, a world soaked in the religious sectarianism of those (almost everyone) who believed that they were right and everyone else was wrong. Milton squares it with his Christian faith like this:

Truth indeed came once into the world with her divine master, and was a perfect shape most glorious to look on; but when he ascended, and his divine apostles after him were laid asleep, there straight arose a wicked race of deceivers, who, as that story goes of the Egyptian Typhon with his conspirators, how they dealt with the god Osiris, took the virgin Truth, hewed her lovely form into a thousand pieces and scattered them to the four winds. From that time since, the sad friends of Truth, such as durst appear, imitating the careful search that Isis made for the mangled body of Osiris, went up and down gathering up limb by limb still as they could find them.

This is as powerful an argument as there can be for pluralism and freedom of debate: if truth is scattered in bits like this, then what others say and write may contain a piece of this precious thing which we have not yet discovered for ourselves. 'We have not found them all' (all the bits of truth, that is), Milton sternly tells his audience of 'lords and commons'. In this he was well ahead of his time; John Stuart Mill develops this idea to great effect in *On Liberty*, which came out more than two and a half centuries later, and the Roman Catholic Church did not really grapple with this concept of pluralism until the Second Vatican Council in the 1960s – some would no doubt argue it has still not really come to terms with it.

But a Very Clever Man – or public intellectual, as I suspect he would call himself – called Stanley Fish famously (famous among those who study these things, anyway) tried to recruit Milton as a *pro*-PC figure in a much-quoted contribution to the PC debate of the early 1990s. Professor Fish is, among many other accomplishments, a Milton scholar, and he opens his essay 'There's No Such Thing as Free Speech and It's a Good Thing, Too' like this: 'Not far from the end of his *Areopagitica*, and after having celebrated the virtues of toleration and unregulated publication in passages that find their way into every discussion of free speech and the First Amendment, John Milton brings himself up short and says, of course, I didn't mean Catholics, them we exterminate.' The passage to which he refers is extremely brief, and it seems almost perverse to single out so slight an interruption to the course of this great river of Miltonic prose, but it is striking; 'I mean not tolerate popery,' Milton writes, 'and open superstition, which as it extirpates all religious and civil supremacies, so itself should be extirpated . . . that also which is impious or evil absolutely against faith or manners no law can possibly permit that intends not to unlaw itself.'

So even one of the greatest advocates of free speech admits the idea of limits. And it is not just Catholicism that Milton is attacking here; he seems to be making the broader point that the law cannot allow the publication of any ideas which are judged to threaten the very basis and purpose of a particular society. Fish uses this as a starting point for joining battle in the debate which was then raging in the United States about those university campus codes. The protection of America's much-vaunted First Amendment only applies to speech which does not cross over into action, he argues, and since all speech (especially the kind of hate speech which the codes were designed to stop) has consequences of some kind the First Amendment does not really mean very much.

When I say that there is no such thing as free speech [he explains], I mean that there is no class of utterances separable from the world of conduct, no 'merely' cognitive expressions whose effects can be confined to some prophylactically sealed area of public discourse. And since it is just such expressions

113

that are privileged by the First Amendment (it is expressions free of certain consequences that are to be freely allowed), there is nothing for the amendment to protect, no items in the category 'free expression'.

The implication of this is that questions about what can and cannot be said should be decided not by reference to abstract principles of free speech ('which don't exist except as a component in a bad argument') but become rather political and pragmatic; we should simply ask, 'Would it be useful to stop people saying this or that?' Fish defends the campus codes because he thinks that 'all things considered, it seems a good thing to chill speech like "nigger", "cunt", "kike", and "faggot" '. And he offers this – somewhat tentative – conclusion: 'I am persuaded that at the present moment, right now, the risk of not attending to hate speech is greater than the risk that by regulating it we will deprive ourselves of valuable insights or slide down the slippery slope towards tyranny.'

Think about that for a moment or two in the context of today's politics. Stanley Fish was writing a decade before 11 September 2001, and it is of course unfair to judge his conclusions in the light of what has happened since then. But that last sentence elegantly encapsulates the attitude many people – including those at the top of the British government – have adopted towards Islam and terrorism. And I think it is profoundly wrong-headed.

In the immediate aftermath of 9/11 Tony Blair sought

to force a clear distinction between the Bin Laden concept of *jihad* and the rest of Islam. Our then prime minister told us that he was travelling with and reading a copy of the Koran, and assured us that the ideology behind the attacks on the United States was a 'distortion' of a peace-loving religion. After a meeting with Muslim leaders in Downing Street he said he would not use the phrase 'Islamic terrorists' because 'What happened in America was not the work of Islamic terrorists; it was not the work of Muslim terrorists. It was the work of terrorists pure and simple.' Whether or not you call it Political Correctness, the approach was grounded in a perfectly reasonable analysis: the vast majority of Muslims are not terrorists, and a responsible government of course wants to avoid exacerbating tensions between them and the rest of society. The Fish formula makes perfect sense at a time of crisis.

What is more, the message went down well with the public, partly because it was the one most of us wanted to hear; people liked being reassured that Islam had nothing to do with terrorism. It chimed with the natural liberal instinct that we owe respect to minorities, and moderate Muslim leaders seemed to approve (there were a couple of pieces in the papers suggesting it might be a tiny bit arrogant for a Christian prime minister to deliver his own *fatwas* on what did or did not constitute authentic Islamic teaching, but they ran very much against the general grain of the coverage). Our journalistic ignorance probably helped Mr Blair's message take root. I remember how difficult we found it to deal with the fact that Bin Laden was a *Sunni* extremist. The limited collective knowledge there was in this country's newsrooms (based on the revolution in Iran and the activities of groups like Hezbollah in Lebanon) had the Shiites down as the group which produced all the crazies. 'Wahabiism' was a word not much used in wine bars, and we were certainly not in a position to pass judgements on the finer points of the theology of *jihad*. The Blair line became the 'received wisdom' – not just in Britain but throughout most of Europe. The Italian prime minister, Silvio Berlusconi, always a reliable reverse barometer of politically correct opinion, got into huge trouble towards the end of that September for suggesting that Western civilisation was superior to that of Islamic countries.

I have described earlier my own H.M. Bateman experience of trying to suggest that the reality of the relationship between Islam and terrorism might not be quite as straightforward as the PC line suggested, but a few frowns from kindly Anglican vicars were as nothing compared to the contumely that rained down on the head of Pope Benedict XVI when he addressed the subject. In a speech at a German university during the summer of 2006, Benedict quoted a fourteenth-century Byzantine emperor who said that the Koran was 'evil and inhuman'. The Pope was promptly burnt in effigy in several Muslim countries, there were anti-Catholic demonstrations all over the Middle

East, and in Somalia an Italian nun was murdered. From the *Today* studio in White City I gave the Archbishop of Cardiff, Peter Smith, a hard time about Benedict's lack of tact – it has since emerged that because the Pope was speaking to his old academic mates at Regensburg he did not think to send the lecture for review at the appropriate Vatican department. Amid all the ruckus the actual content of the papal address got well and truly lost.

A year later the Roman Catholic weekly *The Tablet* published an intriguing piece about the background to Benedict's speech. The Byzantine emperor whom he quoted, Manuel II Palaeologus, was a virtual prisoner of the Ottoman sultan in Ankara at the time of his unfortunate remark, and it was made in the course of his account of a series of discussions he had conducted with a distinguished Muslim scholar on the relationship between religion and reason during the winter of 1390–1. Manuel argued that religion must be based on reason and not on violence, and stated his view that Islam was inherently violent. His Muslim opponent agreed with the first part of that argument, but put forward the case that Islam was in fact the more reasonable of the two religions; Christianity, he suggested, made unreasonable demands on believers by insisting that they love their enemies. Islam, on the other hand, set attainable standards, and that explained the phenomenally swift spread of the younger faith.

I think that the idea of loving your enemies is one of the great ethical glories that the Christian Church has offered the world, but the *muderris*, or Muslim professor of law, had a very good point: the Christian teaching *is* unreasonable, and the Muslim idea of resistance is of course more closely attuned to our natural instincts. I have heard a similar point made by a Palestinian academic in Jerusalem. We were discussing the role of Palestinian Christians in the *intifada*, and he told me that many of them were extremely frustrated by the strange teachings of their church which prevented them from engaging in terrorism and offering themselves as suicide bombers. Quite a lot of Christian teaching runs against reason and logic – that is central to the radicalism peculiar to the New Testament – and the idea that Islam is not only the true faith but also a more rational one than Christianity is an honourable and ancient tradition of Islamic thinking.

This way of looking at Muslim attitudes to violence is both interesting and, it seems to me, absolutely essential to understanding the nature of radical Islam. Of course it does not mean justifying 11 September or the 7 July bombings in London, and of course there is a wide range of opinions within Islam itself about these matters. But if we fail to appreciate that some of the ideas which drive people to turn themselves into human bombs do have a connection with Islam, and that espousing them does not necessarily make you completely mad, we cannot possibly get to grips with the process of radicalisation which is the subject of such endless public soul-searching. It is a little like trying to understand the Inquisition, the Crusades and all the burnings and beheadings which disfigured Europe during the sixteenth and seventeenth centuries while pretending that none of them had anything to do with Christianity. Yet in February 2008 the British government brought out what the *Guardian* called a 'new counter-terrorism phrasebook' which seemed designed to suppress any sense that there might be a link between Islam and the more extreme forms of the religion; it instructed civil servants to avoid the phrases 'Islamic/Islamist/Muslim extremism' for fear of giving offence. The document rather revealingly insisted: 'this is not about political correctness, but effectiveness (in getting across the anti-extremist message)'. To me it suggests a dangerous unwillingness to confront the truth.

We do not, of course, live in a country where the government uses the law to stop people saying things it does not like . . . Or do we? One of the reasons this area is so intriguing is that it has brought together politically correct instincts and the authoritarian instincts which naturally tug at any government's sleeve in a time of crisis. In response to the events of 11 September 2001 the Blair government brought forward a new anti-terrorism bill, and it included a section to make 'incitement to religious hatred' a crime. The House of Lords did not like it and the relevant clauses were excised from the bill. But the government tried again in the Serious Organised Crime and Police Bill of 2005 and, after the general election of that year, again in its Racial and Religious Hatred Bill. The government's position was based very much on the Stanley Fish principle I have outlined above, but over the four and a half years during which this debate was fought out the free speech principles which the professor so cleverly demeans were brought powerfully into play.

All sorts of celebrities who do not usually mix it in political debates weighed in against the idea of a ban on religious hate speech. The comedian Rowan Atkinson worried that it might stop him making good jokes. The writer Salman Rushdie, who of course has good personal reasons for worrying about Islamic ideas of free speech, took the broad historical view.

To me it is further evidence [he wrote of the government's plan] that in Britain, just as in the United States, we may have to fight the battle for the Enlightenment all over again. That battle, you may remember, was about the church's desire to place limits on thought. Diderot's novel *La Religieuse*, with its portrayal of nuns and their behaviour, was deliberately blasphemous. It challenged religious authority, with its indexes and inquisitions, on what it was possible to say. Most of our contemporary ideas about freedom of speech and imagination come from the Enlightenment. But although we may have thought the battle long-since won, if we aren't careful, it is about to be un-won.

Fundamentalist Christians who were worried about spies taking notes during their Sunday services and passing on the spicier passages to the authorities (the 'sermon police' perhaps?) joined in too. It is not often that a piece of legislation forges quite such an odd coalition, with satirical secularists lining up alongside earnest believers, and its oddness perhaps contributed to its effectiveness.

The truth is that religious discourse has *always* included a good measure of language that might be considered an 'incitement to religious hatred'. Even the most liberal-minded believer thinks at some level that his or her lot have got it right and the other lot (or lots) have got it wrong – that is nature of religious belief. If that is what you think, you are bound to want to persuade others of your case, and that means showing why other faiths are wrong as well as why yours is right. Religious leaders cannot avoid being a little bit rude about each other – even if they do it in a very caring way. Some of them actually enjoy being insulting because it gets the doctrinal juices flowing. Perhaps the most ill-tempered religious debate in recent years has been the civil war within Anglicanism over the question of homosexuality; had the government's proposed incitement to religious hatred legislation been in place, a good many of the participants might have been compelled to tone down the language they used about their fellow Anglicans quite a bit.

The battle ended with one of the very rare defeats Tony Blair suffered during his ten years in power. Opponents of the bill successfully insisted that proof of intent to cause religious hatred should be necessary before a prosecution could take place, and they campaigned to add the following clause to the bill: 'Nothing in this Part shall be read or given effect in a way which prohibits or restricts discussion, criticism or expressions of antipathy, dislike or ridicule, insult, or abuse of particular religions or the beliefs or practices of its adherents, or proselytising or urging adherents of a different religion or belief system to cease practising their religion or belief system.' On 31 January 2006 the clause went through in most peculiar circumstances. The Prime Minister was apparently advised by Labour's Chief Whip that the amendment could be defeated without his presence in the lobbies. In fact it passed – by just one vote. It was – with apologies to the Professor – a very significant defeat for the Fishist tendency.

But it was not a total defeat for those who would like to close down discussion – as I discovered uncomfortably close to home when my wife had her collar felt by New Scotland Yard. She works as an executive producer at an independent production company, and the object of the Yard's interest was a documentary they made for the Channel 4 strand *Dispatches*. The reporter Phil Rees, a veteran wanderer in that twilight zone where terrorism and religion mingle (he has written a book called *Dining with Terrorists*), set out to analyse the state of Islam's internal debate about terrorism and to judge the efficacy of, as he put it, 'the government's response: to attempt to silence these voices and prevent Muslims being influenced by radical thoughts'. The debate he outlined revolved around the status of what is known as the 'Covenant of Security'. The Covenant is understood as a kind of social contract between a non-Islamic government and its Muslim citizens: Islam teaches that Muslims should not attack a state in which they live so long as it ensures their safety and gives them freedom to pray. But the radicals claim that in Britain the Covenant was broken when this country sent its troops to fight in Islamic lands, leaving Muslims here in a 'state of war' with their hosts.

The arguments on both sides were laid out with considerable thoroughness and a level of theological detail you do not usually encounter on prime-time television – indeed, the only negative remark my wife received among the generally favourable comments of her peers came from someone who thought that the film had perhaps been a little on the academic side for such a high-profile current affairs slot. The real trouble arose over an interview which Phil Rees conducted with a mysterious figure who appeared under the *nom de guerre* 'Abu Mohammed'. He was wearing sunglasses and a *keffiyeh* arranged to conceal his face. He had, the commentary explained, visited Britain many times in the past but he was now barred from entering the country. Phil Rees told us that he had 'studied at centres of Islamic learning throughout the Middle East' and 'now communicates to followers in Britain through the internet'.

Brandishing a copy of the Koran, Abu Mohammed explained why he believed the group who bombed London on 7 July 2005 had theology on their side: 'It was very justified. Because Allah says if someone committed an aggression against you, you commit aggression against them. If someone transgresses against you, transgress against them in the same way.' The programme did not, of course, suggest that he was right; the point of this was to give a flavour of the sort of messages being given to young Muslims in Britain and of the way the Koran was being used to give those messages Islamic credibility. Phil Rees challenged him over the government's strategy: 'What about what the government says – that people like yourself have misread the faith, that the true faith is one of love, and social cohesion and living together in Britain?' he asked. 'That is not true,' his interviewee insisted, '. . . you have a choice to make . . . calling Allah a liar or calling the British government a liar. I would be very careful in calling Allah a liar.'

Abu Mohammed's performance attracted the attention of the Shadow Home Secretary David Davis, who denounced Channel 4 for putting such views into the public domain, 'This man must never be allowed to appear ranting on our television screens again,' he declared. His fellow Tory MP Philip Davies, a member of the Commons Media and Culture Committee, weighed in with 'It is appalling that an extremist like this should be given a free platform to express his obnoxious views,' and there was an outraged editorial in the *Daily Express*. Rather oddly, the paper quoted the Thatcher government's broadcasting ban on the voices of Gerry Adams and his Sinn Fein colleagues in the 1980s as an example of the way censorship could work against terrorism – oddly, because the ban was made to seem ludicrous when broadcasters began hiring actors to say their words instead.

New Scotland Yard wrote to my wife's company to say that they had received a complaint that 'elements or participants of this production may be in breach of current legislation', and it later emerged that they were referring to the Prevention of Terrorism Act introduced after the London bombings. Section One of the Act deals with 'a statement that is likely to be understood by some or all of the members of the public to whom it is published as a direct or indirect encouragement or other inducement to them to the commission, preparation or instigation of acts of terrorism'. It includes anything that 'glorifies the commission or preparation (whether in the past, in the future or generally)' of terrorist acts, and you can be found guilty of this offence even if you do not actually intend to encourage terrorism but are merely 'reckless as to whether members of the public will be directly or indirectly encouraged or otherwise induced by the statement to commit, prepare or instigate such acts or offences'.

The Metropolitan Police believed that under the Act there was a case to be made against Abu Mohammed because of what he said, and they wanted help in finding him. The outcome of their efforts is, at the time of writing, uncertain, but their letter to my wife's company included what one has to assume was a Freudian slip – and a very revealing one. 'Please provide,' it said, 'an unedited version of both the documentary and the interview with "Abu Muhammed". This is required to negate any allegation of bias on your company or its agent's part.' Bias? When, pray, did questions of journalistic balance become the responsibility of the constabulary? Despite all I have written about the danger of using loose language, this really does deserve the description 'Political Correctness gone mad'. It is a sharp reminder that authoritarian instincts are alive and well here, just as they are in the United States.

Section One of the Prevention of Terrorism Act 2005 would, I suspect, have outraged the second author on the Chief Rabbi's reading list. Like Milton – and of course Professor Fish – John Stuart Mill does accept that there have to be some limits on freedom of speech, and he deals with the question of incitement head on. 'An opinion that corn-dealers are starvers of the poor, or that private property is robbery,' he writes, 'ought to be unmolested when simply circulated through the press, but may justly incur punishment when delivered orally to an excited mob assembled before the house of a corn-dealer, or when handed about among the same mob in the form of a placard.' But, in sharp contrast to Professor

Fish, Mill is disposed to put as much as possible into the box marked 'protected under the right to freedom of speech' and very little in the category of speech which is judged to cross over into the sphere of action and can therefore be regulated. 'Strange it is,' he declares, in a neat inversion of the Fish formula, 'that men should admit the validity of the arguments for free discussion, but object to their being "pushed to the extreme"; not seeing that unless the reasons are good for an extreme case, they are not good for any case.'

And he makes two points which have particular relevance to Islamic justifications for violence of the kind I have just been discussing. The first is that we become lazy and complacent in our thinking when our beliefs are not subject to challenge, so even discussion of ideas that are untrue or repulsive – like those espoused by the radical Islamist in my wife's film – is beneficial; the effort and thought required to rebut them reinvigorates our own beliefs and reminds us of why we hold the views we do. The second relates to the tone in which debate is conducted. Mill argues that invective and 'vituperative language' are most dangerous when used in support of the 'prevailing view' – what we might these days called received wisdom or establishment opinion – because then it 'really does deter people from expressing contrary opinions'. If it is used by dissenters, the argument runs, it usually alienates people, and therefore can be taken much less seriously as a weapon of debate. 'If it were necessary to choose,' Mill states, 'there would be much more need to discourage offensive attacks on infidelity than on religion. It is obvious, however, that law and authority have no business in restraining either.' It seems reasonable to assume that Mill – who was an MP for a while – would not have voted for the Racial and Religious Hatred Bill in the form originally proposed by the government.

Indeed, reading *On Liberty* is a slightly eerie experience because so many of its targets echo today's anti-PC rhetoric. Mill excoriates what we would now call nanny statism, telling 'intrusively pious members of society' to 'mind their own business'. He insists that we should all be allowed to get drunk if we want to (as long as we do not inconvenience anyone else by doing so) and dismisses the campaign of the virtuous Victorians who were then trying to ban the sale of alcohol as 'monstrous'. The case he advances for the free sale of poison would make him a convincing twenty-first-century smokers' champion: he accepts that poison bottles should be clearly labelled but argues against any further restriction on the sale of such dangerous material because

When there is not a certainty, but only a danger of mischief, no one but the person himself can judge of the sufficiency of the motive which may prompt him to incur the risk: in this case, therefore (unless he is a child, or delirious, or in some state of excitement or absorption incompatible with the full use of the reflecting faculty), he ought, I conceive, to be only warned of the danger; not forcibly prevented from exposing himself to it.

Perhaps we should not be surprised to find echoes of our own PC World in an essay written a century and a half ago, because Mill warns us that the closing down of debate is a recurrent danger. While most of us accept the theory that we might sometimes be wrong we find it very difficult to admit that in practice, and almost all of us, in every age, tend towards the assumption that we have arrived at a unique and near complete level of wisdom – even though, as Mill points out, 'ages are no more infallible than individuals; every age having held many opinions which subsequent ages have deemed not only false but absurd'. Because of that there is always a temptation to censor opinion and speech which challenges what Mill calls 'prevailing opinion' – whether through laws or the sort of moral pressure implied in the phrase 'Political Correctness': 'So natural to mankind is intolerance in whatever they really care about,' he declares. And, like a number of those I have quoted in this chapter, John Stuart Mill believed that the greatest threat often comes from people with the best of intentions; citing the deaths of Socrates and Jesus to illustrate what dreadful wrongs can be done in the name of the 'prevailing opinion', he describes those responsible as 'not bad men – not worse than people commonly are, but rather the contrary; men who possessed in full, or somewhat more than full measure, the religious, moral, and patriotic feelings of their time and people'. Reading John Stuart Mill did make me think that the sins of our PC World are merely the most recent expression of a very ancient form of human folly.

*On Liberty* stands out from most of the other texts I have quoted because it is completely free of any sense of partisanship. Even in the *Areopagitica* you are left with a strong sense of where the author is, as they say, 'coming from', and that is certainly true of the modern books to which I have referred. John Stuart Mill takes delight in contrariness; like a treasure hunter who seeks to increase his pleasure by searching in unlikely places, he looks for his slivers of fractured truth in wild and eccentric opinions. So let me close this chapter with some counter-intuitive views from my colleague Peter White which I think bear on an important truth.

You might have thought that as a champion of disabled rights Peter would enjoy covering positive stories about disabled people – the sort of reporting which can provide examples of their often admirable achievements. In fact, the two stories he singled out for special mention during our conversation did precisely the reverse. One was about a doping scandal involving East European bench-pressing competitors at the 2000 Paralympics in Sydney. The other was about an alleged car-trading scam by a group of prominent disabled people who were accused of profiteering from their exemption from VAT on disability-modified vehicles (they were said to be reconverting the cars for normal use and selling them on the open market). As a journalist, Peter of course relished the stories because they attracted attention (the doping scandal made the lead slot on *Today*). But as someone concerned with disability, he was also pleased because the stories served as such a vivid illustration of the principle that disabled people should not be treated as in any sense a class set apart. 'It showed that we can cheat too,' he said, 'just like anyone else.'

His comment touches on a scratchy bird's nest of questions that lies just below the surface of many conversations about Political Correctness. I noted in Chapter 1 that the emergence of PC as a big public issue has coincided with the arrival of a politics of identity in place of a politics of ideology. That is probably the most significant difference between our PC World and the climate in which John Stuart Mill wrote a century and a half ago, and we still have not quite worked out the implications of the change. Should minorities focus on being treated in the same way as everyone else – which seems to be Peter's instinct – or are there some who have been so badly treated in the past that membership today carries an entitlement to privilege? Is minority status entirely self-defining, or do the rest of us have to sign up to the idea that a particular group has a right to claim it? And what happens when the rights of two groups of people who regard themselves as minorities come into conflict?

# 4

# My rights in a PC World

We are . . . so busy slicing and dicing ourselves into ever-smaller groups that the ties that bind are fraying. If I may paraphrase John Donne, 'No minority is an island, entire unto itself.' Yet multicultural (and other) special interest groups are proliferating at a disconcerting rate, fragmenting the whole and creating increasingly balkanized discourse communities as the mania for identity politics takes root.

Blaise Cronin, *Jeremiad Jottings*

Consider the following case studies:

## Item 1

In December 2006 Tosca, a polar bear who had retired from her role as a circus performer and was being cared for in Berlin Zoo, gave birth to a male cub, which she rejected. The zoo staff named him Knut (pronounced as in 'sweet as a . . .') and bottle-fed him. No doubt he was, in the fullness of time, destined to grow into a dangerous brute, but as a cub he was almost impossibly charming and quickly became something of a Berlin celebrity. He even attracted the attention of Annie Leibovitz, the distinguished photographer whose subjects range from Andy Warhol and John Lennon to – famously – the Queen; she took Knut's portrait for a campaign on global warming.

But when Knut was some three months old he became the centre of the sort of controversy that could only happen in a PC World, and it caught the attention of newspaper editors everywhere. The popular German weekly magazine *Spiegel* reported the story like this: 'Animal rights activists . . . aren't so enthralled with the polar bear baby. They are concerned that Knut, who is being raised by human hand after his mother rejected him, is in danger of losing touch with the bear necessities. Some would like to see him dead.' The story was based on comments from an animal rights activist named Frank Albrecht, who declared that 'Raising him by hand is not appropriate to the species but rather a blatant violation of animal welfare laws . . . In actual fact, the zoo needs to kill the bear cub.' The director of another zoo said, 'The animal will be fixated on his keeper and not be a "real" polar bear', and *Spiegel* reported that 'baby zoo animals have been killed for the same reason in the past. Two-day-old baby sloth Hugo was put down by lethal injection in Leipzig Zoo at the end of last year, sparking emotional protests.'

The mass-circulation newspaper *Bild* ran Mr Albrecht's comments under the headline 'Will Sweet Knut Be Killed by Injection?' and followed up the story with pictures of young children demonstrating at the zoo with placards reading 'Knut Must Live' and 'We Love Knut'. The paper quoted a certain Alexander, aged four (and, it would seem, precociously articulate): 'I thought animal rights activists were supposed to protect animals and didn't want to kill them,' he apparently declared, adding, in a judgement that will no doubt have summed up the feelings of many readers, 'They are really silly!'

But there was to be a happy ending – for Knut at any rate. Berlin Zoo was unimpressed by the politically correct line from those 'animal activists', and remained determined that Knut should live. On the day of his eagerly awaited first public appearance at the zoo (in late March 2007), the *Daily Mail* reported that

He delighted the crowd by clambering over a log and sniffing curiously at the legs of his handler, Thomas Doerflein, who feeds him three times a day with a bottle. 'We want Knut! We want Knut!' chanted a group of youngsters allowed in after protesting against demands by animal rights activists that the bear should be given a lethal injection rather than be subjected to the indignity of life as a domesticated animal.

The upshot of the episode was to make Knut an international superstar. Mr Albrecht was rather less fortunate.

His life, reported *Spiegel*, 'appears to be in more danger than Knut's. "I've received a whole lot of threatening e-mails and phone calls," Albrecht told the German news agency DDP . . . One e-mail, he claimed, warned him that he should watch his back. Other callers and e-mailers suggested that he have himself put down.'

## Item 2

On 30 September 2007 the *Sunday Times* carried the headline 'Muslim Checkout Staff Get an Alcohol Opt-out Clause'. The story reported that the supermarket chain Sainsbury's had introduced a policy to allow Muslim checkout staff to excuse themselves from handling alcohol when serving customers. It described the routine followed by Mustapha, a checkout worker at the Sainsbury's branch at Swiss Cottage in north London; 'Each time a bottle or can of alcohol comes along the conveyor belt in front of him, Mustapha either swaps places discreetly with a neighbouring attendant or raises his hand so that another member of staff can come over and pass the offending items in front of the scanner before he resumes work.' But the paper also recorded that 'Some of the staff delegated to handle the drink for Mustapha are themselves obviously Muslim, including women in *hijab* head coverings.'

Islamic teaching on the consumption of alcohol is clear, but the question of whether Muslims can trade in or handle alcohol is a source of much debate and disagreement among Muslim scholars. And Islamic reaction to the new Sainsbury's policy was somewhat mixed. Ghayasuddin Siddiqui, director of the Muslim Institute and leader of the Muslim Parliament, did not like it: 'This is some kind of over-enthusiasm. One expects professional behaviour from people working in a professional capacity and this shows lack of maturity.' Inayat Bunglawala, the assistant secretary-general of the Muslim Council of Britain, told the *Daily Mail*: 'By selling alcohol you are not committing a sin. You are just doing the job you are paid for. Muslim employees have a duty to their employer and in supermarkets most people would accept that in selling alcohol you are merely passing it through a checkout. That is hardly going to count against you on the day of judgement.'

Some of the concern expressed by members of the Muslim establishment (if it makes any sense to talk about such a thing) reflected a worry that the measure would provoke an anti-Muslim backlash. Ibrahim Mogra, who chairs the inter-faith committee at the Muslim Council of Britain, said that 'Muslims should look at the allowances within Muslim law to enable them to be better operating employees and not be seen as rather difficult to cater for.' The *Sunday* programme on Radio Four broadcast a lively discussion between Ashgar Bukhari, one of the moving spirits behind the Muslim Public Affairs Committee, and Humera Khan of the trend-setting

Muslim publication *Q Magazine*. Khan expressed reservations about the Sainsbury's policy on the grounds that its logic raised all sorts of questions about other minority groups; what about Jews selling pork, for example, or Catholics working in a chemist who are asked for condoms? Bukhari heartily endorsed what the supermarket chain was doing, and dismissed objections to it as bigotry. 'It doesn't matter what the Muslims do,' he said, 'someone is always ready to single them out and bash them and make a hoo-ha out of it.'

## Item 3

In the summer of 2007 Radio Four's hugely respected current affairs strand *File on Four* broadcast an edition on the subject of so-called 'honour killings' in Britain. Angus Stickler, an old-school investigative journalist with a string of radio awards to his name, provided harrowing details of a depressingly long list of cases in which young women from (mostly) Muslim communities had been pursued – sometimes to the point of death – by members of their own families. This transcript of an interview with the police officer involved in one of the cases provides a flavour of the kind of evidence he had gathered.

*Stickler*:  Detective Inspector Brent Hyatt was the senior investigating officer in the murder of Heshu Jones, a Kurdish girl killed by her Muslim father for daring to date a boy without his consent, bringing dishonour on the family. She was imprisoned in the family home. Forensics show he attacked her first in the bedroom. She fled to the bathroom, locking the door. He forced his way in.

*Hyatt*:   Seeking refuge in that bathroom, she must have been in absolute terror. I suspect that the reason why she fled from her bedroom when she was first attacked to the bathroom and didn't flee out of the front door was because she was locked in the property and knew that she couldn't escape. She was stabbed seventeen times, you know, the head, the neck, the back, the arms, the chest. Both of her lungs were punctured, her collar-bone was broken, her throat was cut . . . the blows were delivered with such force that the knife penetrated, for instance, right through both sides of her forearms. The knife was twisted, bent, and the tip was broken off of it with the ferocity of that attack.

*Stickler*:   All at the hands of her own father?

*Hyatt*:   Of course, yes, absolutely right – at the hands of her own father, who showed absolutely no remorse whatsoever.

Following the Heshu Jones case, Scotland Yard set up a group to address the phenomenon of honour killings and Brent Hyatt was recruited to the team. In 2002 he began giving a training course on the subject. But the course was put on hold after complaints about its content. Angus Stickler attended one of the sessions (which were re-instated after a 'pause', during which they were subject to investigation) and afterwards he interviewed Inspector Hyatt about what had happened.

*Stickler*:   . . . did people try and stop you saying what you've said here today?
*Hyatt*:   Erm, there were people that objected to some of the input that we've had here today.
*Stickler*:   What did they object to?
*Hyatt*:   They objected to the content of some of the presentation and I think their concern, if I can summarise it, was that this presentation was in some way Islamophobic, racist or anti-Kurdish.

Stickler further reported that 'Around the same time that Inspector Hyatt's training programme was put on hold, a review of 117 suspicious deaths was halted. Out of twenty-two analysed, nine were believed to be honour-based murders. Political correctness, we've been told – by former and serving senior staff – brought the drive to tackle honour crime to a near standstill.'

There are very obviously significant differences in the seriousness of these three case studies, but they share certain underlying characteristics which we may – at the risk of straying into pomposity – describe as some of the 'structures' of Political Correctness. Forgive me for lapsing into socio-babble at this point, but a couple of slightly bogus academic-sounding categories might help us understand what has really gone wrong.

In each case a politically correct view is taken by representatives of what you might describe as a 'power group' – in other words, a group which has historically held power over what I shall call their 'victim groups'. The power group representatives are Mr Albrecht (representing human beings), Sainsbury's (representing big business) and the unnamed PC PCs, DCIs and so on (representing the police). The respective 'victim groups' are zoo animals, Muslims and religious and ethnic minorities in general. In all the cases the power group representatives have admirable motives: they are trying to compensate for past injustices. But each of them has made a judgement about the interests of their respective victim groups without seeking a full range of opinion from those they are trying to help.

Thus Mr Albrecht evidently believes he is able to make a judgement about what is in Knut's best interests, irrespective of Knut's own views. Obviously these are somewhat difficult to explore in any depth, and I suppose it is just possible that if we could understand polar bear we might discover that Knut's charming squealing noises actually meant 'give me the needle now'. But because the cute little cub took to his keeper's bottle with such enthusiasm it seems reasonable to infer that his instinct for self-preservation was strong. Sainsbury's is the least culpable in this regard, because it does appear that the supermarket was responding to a genuine demand, but, as I have reported above, the wisdom of its action was questioned by a number of prominent figures in the group it believed it was helping. Finally – and most importantly – those police officers concerned about the politically correct pitfalls involved in investigating honour crime plainly had not sought the views of the desperate young women featured in Angus Stickler's programme – young women who were, of course, themselves members of religious and ethnic minorities.

In all three cases the impression left is precisely the reverse of that which was intended: the power groups are once again telling those under them, 'We know what's good for you.'

The good news – and it is very good news which should not be forgotten – is that in all these cases common sense ultimately proved a more powerful force than politically correct thinking. Berlin Zoo did not kill Knut. We do not have to queue for hours in the supermarket because the checkout counters have become Babel Towers of noisy minority demands for special treatment. And, again most importantly, Inspector Hyatt resumed his courses, Angus Stickler broadcast his programme (remember that next time you hear someone complain that the BBC is too PC) and these days not many people think it is 'culturally insensitive' to investigate honour crime.

But the bad news is that these three case studies reflect a more general collective moral and intellectual funk about how to deal with the politics of identity I alluded to at the end of the last chapter.

I have suggested earlier that the rise of identity politics was closely tied up with the collapse of the Soviet Union and consequent discrediting of Communism as an ideological system – developments which in turn led to the passing of the old, familiar system of ideology politics. If 9 November 1989, the day the Berlin Wall came down, was one seminal date in this process, 11 September 2001 was almost as important because of the way it has driven the direction the process has taken more recently.

Many Muslims felt understandably threatened in the aftermath of the Al Qaeda attacks and quickly concluded they needed people who could articulate their concerns. At the same time Western governments – certainly our own – were looking for responsible Muslim leaders with whom they could have a real conversation about the appropriate response to what had happened in New York and Washington. In Britain these dynamics created something that Islam here had never really had before; a number of Muslim 'names' – such as Iqbal Sacranie and Zaki Badawi – who suddenly became recognised as the legitimate national voices of their religion. At the same time various bodies with official-sounding titles like 'The Muslim Council of Britain' and 'The Muslim Parliament' acquired new prominence as newspapers and broadcasters looked desperately for individuals and organisations they could use as credible sources of 'Islamic opinion'. All of these people and organisations were treated as if they could speak on behalf of 'the community' – the fact that we all now understand that phrase to mean 'British Muslims' represents the triumph of a telling elliptical construction.

We now know that these people and bodies, admirable though many of them may be, do not in fact speak for the whole of 'the community'. It turns out that – surprise, surprise – Islamic opinion is divided on some really quite profound issues – just like Christianity. As editor of Radio Four's Religion and Ethics flagship *Sunday* (and thus one of my bosses) Amanda Hancox has the job of weighing up the credibility of guests who appear on the programme; she says the task is greatly complicated by the fact that Islam simply does not have a tradition of the sort of leadership structures we are used to dealing with in a culture with Christian roots. There is no Islamic pope or archbishop of Canterbury. The phenomenon of the 'spokespersons' for British Muslims who have become so prominent is really an artificial construct built to meet the very particular circumstances of the world since 9/11.

And that carries certain risks. The first is that we shall be taken by surprise when confronted by a strand of Islamic thought that does not chime with the message we have heard from those impressively titled and acronymically decorated spokespersons we have been listening to so closely – when, for example, the religion we have been so firmly told has no connection with terrorism is used as a justification for violence in the video recorded by Mohammed Sidique Khan, the leader of the 7 July London bombers.

The second is that it changes the way British Muslims think about themselves; if you hear your self-styled leaders talking constantly about 'the community' you are likely to think of your 'community' identity before anything else – including your national identity. The idea of your separateness and distinctiveness becomes sharper and more important.

This may not always be a bad thing; I am perfectly happy to admit to having a strong sense of a Catholic identity alongside my British identity, and part of it is certainly that English Catholics inherit a distinctive history and set of cultural attitudes. I have even had it suggested to me by the Euro-sceptic former editor of a national newspaper that being brought up as a Roman Catholic is more likely to make one sympathetic to the European Union. But by and large I think these differences enrich rather than diminish my sense of being part of the society in which I live – and the arguments which really divided Catholics from their Protestant fellow-citizens in this country have of course long since lost their dangerous edge.

But distinctiveness *can* also be dangerous, and the Angus Stickler programme I have quoted from earlier provides a very vivid illustration of why. The programme included an interview with a spokesman for the Muslim Council of Britain who stated – with some passion – that

honour killings had nothing to do with Islam and are a
'cultural practice'; it is, of course, very difficult to think
of anything in the Koran that could possibly justify this
ghastly tradition. But one of the most telling contributions in the programme came from Nazir Afzal, director
of prosecutions for the Crown Prosecution Service in West
London and the man in charge of prosecutions for honour
crime for the CPS as a whole. 'You have many second-
generation youths who have this exaggerated concept of
what home is like,' said Mr Afzal, who is himself a Muslim.

They get their identity and their ethnicity from these traditions.
We know they are bizarre and they're outdated and they are
quite horrific traditions, [but] they feel very strongly that the
way you treat your women is a demonstration of your commitment to radicalism and radical thought and extremist thought
and they are proud of the fact that they will treat their women
in a certain way.

Think a little about the process he is describing here: it
is one in which all sorts of things are being jumbled up,
balled together under the pressure to define yourself in
opposition to the world in which you find yourself; culture,
ethnic identity and radical religion are stirred into a cocktail labelled 'distinctiveness'. In the last chapter I traced
the liberal opposition to the government's proposal for
religious hatred legislation; at its heart lies a distinction
between a quality like skin colour – which you cannot

change – and religious belief, which ought in theory to be susceptible to debate and challenge. But for the young men Mr Afzal is describing, that distinction has no real meaning; their beliefs and 'cultural practices' – including being vile to women – have become almost as immutable as the colour of their skins. To the extent that this process has been driven by the turbulent social currents that have swirled around us since the attacks of 9/11, it is not entirely fanciful to see the young women in Angus Stickler's programme as Osama Bin Laden's victims.

And, like the proverbial stone thrown into a calm pond, the impact of 9/11 has sent its waves through other faith communities which had until that dreadful day been settling comfortably into British society. Britain's Sikhs were, of course, one of the first groups to ask to be treated as a special case; the famous 'turban campaigns' began in 1959 when a Manchester Sikh, G.S.S. Sagar, demanded the right to wear the traditional headgear while working as a bus conductor. But those battles were fought (and, largely, won) several decades ago. In more recent years the Sikh national 'voice' has been a very mellow one – literally so, in the sense that Indarjit Singh of *Thought for the Day* has been the most prominent Sikh spokesman. But with 9/11 and the new focus on Islam's place in Britain, young Sikhs began to shout a bit more loudly about the need for Sikhs' rights too. The Sikh Federation (UK) was established in 2003 'with the aim of giving Sikhs a stronger political voice'. The piece published on the organisation's website during the period of national shock and mourning in the aftermath of the London bombings of 2005 is revealingly eccentric in its 'take' on what mattered then:

Those of you that have followed the Federation's public statements and press releases on the tragic events of Thursday 7 July will be aware we have expressed our surprise and annoyance of the almost complete absence of Sikh representation and coverage. Following a complaint by the Federation to Ken Livingstone's office regarding his glaring omission of any mention of Sikhs it was a pleasant surprise to see five turbaned Sikhs in the 200 or so present at City Hall. Similarly, the Sikh Missionary Society (UK) was represented at the London Memorial Garden event . . .

Throughout the week Sikhs continued to take part in other events to guarantee Sikh visibility. Whether this be the community reassurance event at the Queen Elizabeth II Conference Centre on Monday, 10 Downing Street and the Sikh Lobby Day at the Houses of Parliament on Tuesday, various meetings with the police at New Scotland Yard, providing interviews to BBC News 24, ITN TV News and various national radio stations, [the] Vigil in Trafalgar Square on Thursday and Sir Ian Blair's visit to Dasmesh Darbar Gurdwara on Friday.

Whilst Sikhs have had better representation in the last week than in the first few days following the tragic events of Thursday 7 July there remains a problem of sufficient coverage and acknowledgement of Sikhs in political circles. All Sikhs – young and old, educated or less educated, leaders and non-leaders – must wake up to the fact that we will only really count if we 'shout' loud enough in the right places.

Britain's Catholics have been battling with the British establishment for rather longer, and they have learnt that raising your voice like that at a time of national tragedy is considered bad form and does not help your cause very much. But they too have been shaken by the 9/11 effect. Many of them resent the very phrase 'faith communities' which has become such common currency since then – if you think of yourself as a member of the One True Holy Catholic and Apostolic Church, the idea that you can be bundled up with everyone else as simply one 'faith community' among many is more than a little irritating.

What is more, this dramatic change in the religious weather has hit British Catholics just as they were beginning to enjoy the sense that they had recovered their place in the nation's life, settling into that comfortable conviction I have referred to that the really dangerous divisions which separate them from their fellow citizens have lost their edge. One of the greatest legacies of the late Cardinal Basil Hume was to make Catholics feel at ease with British society and British society feel at ease with Catholics. Charles Wookey was a close adviser to Hume and is now a senior official working for the Bishops' Conference of England and Wales. This is an extract from a recent lecture he gave, in which he reflected that Catholics today are regarded – once again – as being in some way 'peculiar' and unsettling to those around them.

Why has this happened now? Why are we suddenly weird? Part of the answer . . . is the rise of scary religion – by which I mean 9/11, 7/7 and religious fundamentalism in all its forms. I believe the West is still shaking in the aftershocks of this seismic event. It had immense symbolic power far beyond the immediate tragedy and that is far from fully absorbed even now. The terrorists claimed they were acting in the name of their religion. It exploded the myth that a totally open religious pluralism and the acceptance of all things 'religious' were possible. And in a society like ours, where already Christianity had long lost its prominent role, and many people saw religion and faith as one thing, that 'one thing' suddenly becomes not a social good, but a problem . . .

Religion was already strange, but now it is palpably dangerous. Of course much of the focus of this is Islam, but with a combination of ignorance of faiths and of history I don't think everyone makes these distinctions between faiths. And then the language of the public square lumps all faiths and religions together. The inclusive and politically correct language of 'faith communities' blurs many distinctions, and encourages everyone to think that they're all the same. 'Religion' for many people is just one thing. Anyone who is religious is involved in the same strange activity. Suddenly as Catholics we can find ourselves being expected to justify and defend religion per se, as if we too were being judged and tarnished by anything bad done in the name of any faith.

All that chimes perfectly sensibly with my own analysis of what has been happening – but then I am 'one of them', so I suppose it would. If I put on my BBC reporter's hat – the one that helps me see what people in the 'public square' might think – I can well imagine that others might hear the less harmonious sound of jangled nerves. Not so very long ago the leaders of most religions would probably have been united in the view that secularism and indifference posed the greatest threat to the survival of faith in a society like ours. Today the scene looks very different; everyone seems to be – if you will forgive the mixed metaphor – simultaneously shouting from the rooftops for special treatment and heading for the bunker of distinctiveness.

And at the same time the more general trend towards 'slicing and dicing ourselves into ever-smaller groups' – in the words of the conservative cultural critic Blaise Cronin which I have quoted at the beginning of this chapter – continues apace. There is a school of thought which says this is something to be celebrated. Sir Trevor Phillips, who chairs the Equality Commission, the new, over-arching body charged with the task of fighting discrimination, wrote this in his introduction to the 2007 *Final Report of the Equalities Review*:

for good historical reasons, much of recent generations' effort to make Britain fairer has been focused on prevention; in particular, stopping the abuse of power by both individuals and institutions to discriminate against people on specific grounds – gender, ethnicity, and disability. In the past few years, disquiet about attitudes to sexual orientation, religion or belief, transgender, and age have been added to that list. We expect other groups, such as carers, to become equally significant in the years ahead.

That is a kind of answer to the criticism implied in Blaise Cronin's very loaded choice of words; the process of slicing ourselves up into groups is really a way of slicing up – and ultimately, thereby, eliminating – the very existence of discrimination itself. At least so the theory goes.

The *Final Report of the Equalities Review* was commissioned as an audit of equality in the Britain of the twenty-first century and it is, judged by the standards of quango-sponsored reports of this kind, a clearly written – and, indeed, thorough – attempt to address some very profound questions, the big one of 'what is equality?' included. But precisely because it is so clearly written it reveals the weaknesses as well as the strengths of the identity-based philosophy that informs it. Here is the way it describes recent developments in thinking about discrimination:

The insight that discrimination might not be restricted solely to consciously prejudicial acts by one individual against another was a profound breakthrough in all aspects of equality. In the field of disability, the development of the 'social model of disability' began to change the way in which people thought about equality overall. This view held that disadvantages faced by disabled people arose less from their particular impairment, and more from the way that society constructed (often literally) the world and erected barriers. This meant that campaigning efforts shifted from a focus on a disabled person's particular impairment(s) to the action that should be taken to remove the barriers faced by disabled persons in everyday life.

It is an incontrovertible fact – and one worthy of unqualified celebration – that the daily lives of disabled people have been greatly improved by the Disability Discrimination Acts of 1995 and 2005, which were the legislative expression of the 'social model' to which this passage refers. It is equally incontrovertible – at least so it seems to me – that the view 'that disadvantages faced by disabled people arose less from their particular impairment, and more from the way that society constructed (often literally) the world and erected barriers' is based on a falsehood. If you place a blind person in a Rousseau-esque state of nature or on Robinson Crusoe's island, he or she will, surely, be disadvantaged next to someone who can see in the same circumstances. Of course society can and often does make things more difficult for disabled people and of course there is a social duty to make things easier for them – of course, indeed, disabled people should be able to expect that *as of right*, and not as some gracious concession. But none of that requires us to accept a version of reality which simply is not true.

The review carries one table which breaks down educational achievement by races listed as 'White British, Traveller of Irish Heritage, Gypsy/Roma, Mixed – White/Caribbean, Pakistani, Bangladeshi, Black Caribbean, Black African, Black Other', another on population growth among ethnic minorities which excludes the Travellers of Irish Heritage and the Gypsies/Romas as specific groups (does this mean they do not count as ethnic minorities?) but includes the Chinese, and still another (on GCSE passes) which includes all of these groups and adds Mixed White and Asian, Mixed White and Black African, and Irish. Like Trevor Phillips's introduction, the body of the report welcomes the way that 'the pattern of social change, activist campaigning and consequent legislation has steadily spread the reach of equality legislation and policy to new groupings of people'. As an illustration of this process the report cites successful lobbying for employment rights by transgender people (or 'trans people', to use its shorthand), the 'emergence of British Muslims as a group who are widely recognised to be systematically disadvantaged' and the way 'carers' have joined the list of those benefiting from this trend; 'carers and carers' organisations', it says, have 'found a voice as well as increasing sympathy for their cause. The right to flexible working, for example, will be extended to carers in the next few months.'

Does it really make sense to talk about all these groups in the same way? When – to take the argument back across the Atlantic for a moment – we refer to a group of people as African Americans, we immediately evoke a huge and rich tapestry of shared history which includes those most compelling of stories, transportation, slavery and the struggle for civil rights. Black Caribbean people living in Britain can lay claim to a similar shared history, and many of our communities which trace their origins to the Indian subcontinent have the same kind of sense of a shared historical and cultural legacy. But carers? That category is likely to include almost all of us at one time or another – black, white and indeed any cocktail of skin colour and faith community you care to imagine. There are certain, very particular ways in which we may, when we are carers, have a common interest (in rather the way members of a trade union do), but does it really make sense to talk about us as the possessors of a common identity?

Two things struck me about the way the *Final Report of the Equalities Review* dealt with the question of identity. The first is that many of the new categories of people seeking redress for discrimination are actually 'categories of convenience' rather than anything else: groups of people who can come together in a useful way to achieve a particular economic, legal or social objective but do not actually have any deep or long-lasting common bond that you could call a shared identity. The second is that as more and more of us merrily break the old boundaries between races and between religions in our love-lives and breeding habits, the more difficult – and less meaningful – it becomes to draw up the sort of lists of achievement or disadvantage I have quoted above; the report notes, in a striking statistic, that the 'number of mixed race births in 2003–4 greatly exceeded the number of births within any of the other non-White groups'.

Might those two factors mean that identity politics will – like the state in a Marxist utopia – eventually wither away? I do not know, but let me offer you another case study – one that sheds light on both the value and the limitations of an identity-based approach to political questions.

Here is an extract from a piece written by the Nobel Prize-winning black American author Toni Morrison in the *New Yorker* in October 1998. The article is an analysis of the public reaction to Bill Clinton as a result of the Monica Lewinsky affair, and she writes that 'the single consistent sound to emerge is a howl of revulsion'.

But revulsion against what? [the piece continues] What is being violated, ruptured, defiled? The bedroom? The Oval Office? The voting booth? The fourth grade? Marriage vows? The flag? Whatever answer is given, underneath the national embarrassment churns a disquiet turned to dread and now anger.

African-American men seemed to understand it right away. Years ago, in the middle of the Whitewater investigation, one heard the first murmurs: white skin notwithstanding, this is our first black President. Blacker than any actual black person who could ever be elected in our children's lifetime. After all, Clinton displays almost every trope of blackness: single-parent household, born poor, working-class, saxophone-playing, McDonald's-and-junk-food-loving boy from Arkansas. And when virtually all the African-American Clinton appointees began, one by one, to disappear, when the President's body, his privacy, his unpoliced sexuality became the focus of the persecution, when he was metaphorically seized and bodysearched, who could gainsay these black men who knew whereof they spoke? The message was clear: 'No matter how smart you are, how hard you work, how much coin you earn for us, we will put you in your place or put you out of the place you have somehow, albeit with our permission, achieved. You will be fired from your job, sent away in disgrace, and – who knows? – maybe sentenced and jailed to boot. In short, unless you do as we say (i.e. assimilate at once), your expletives belong to us.'

Is this a brilliant insight or complete gibberish? Both, really.

It is certainly a very clever means of illuminating the passion generated by the debate about Bill Clinton which divided America at that time. Clinton polarised America in a way it is difficult for non-Americans to understand; we tend to be tone deaf to the kind of all-American melodies – social, generational, religious and political – which clashed in that great cacophonous symphony of public howling which erupted when America tried to impeach its president over a stained dress. During the 1996 presidential campaign I crossed the United States for the BBC's *Panorama* programme to address the puzzle of a man who had – as a draft-dodger and self-confessed adulterer – broken all the taboos of American public life, yet seemed to be floating so effortlessly towards a second term. Part of the answer to the Clinton conundrum undoubtedly lay in Toni Morrison's idea that he was, in some mystical way, the first black president; he spoke to America's dispossessed because they saw him as one of their own.

But of course no amount of Nobel Prize-winning metaphorical gymnastics can actually make Bill Clinton 'black', and the conceit only tells one part of the Clinton story. He may have looked black to African Americans in the United States, but he certainly will not have seemed that way to those Africans in Somalia who found themselves on the receiving end of the Commander-in-Chief's attentions during the Clinton administration's adventures there. Looking at a figure like Bill Clinton through the lens of identity politics can be very useful in one way but not at all useful in another.

Withering or not, there is a curious self-dicing dynamic in the way identity politics have been developing. As groups judged worthy of special attention proliferate, so too does the risk that their interests will cut across one another. I picked up a hint of this while reading an essay about the very PC subject of date rape in a relatively early collection of essays about Political Correctness (*War of Words*, which was published in 1994). After discussing the practice of rape in Bosnia during the war there, the writer Linda Grant records what she sees as the surprisingly enlightened position which is taken by 'even mullahs in mosques in Zagreb'. She probably means Sarajevo rather than Zagreb (which is the capital of Catholic Croatia) but the significant point is that she clearly felt comfortable referring to Muslim leaders in such a dismissive way; being nice about Muslims was not a PC requirement in those days. Now that it is, we are similarly confronted with the spectacle of some Muslims being un-PC about other PC-protected species. When Sir Iqbal Sacranie of the Muslim Council of Britain attacked civil partnership and told the *PM* programme on Radio Four that homosexuality was 'unacceptable', he was investigated by the Metropolitan Police. The veteran gay campaigner Peter Tatchell, remarked that it was 'tragic for one minority to attack another minority'. He added, 'Both the Muslim and gay communities suffer prejudice and discrimination . . . We should stand together to fight Islamophobia and homophobia.'

If you live on a sand of constantly shifting identities you can find yourself sinking. One of the most significant ways in which identity politics have changed in Britain over the past twenty years has been the new nationalism of the peoples that make up the United Kingdom. We have thought of ourselves in all sorts of ways over the centuries, but in a PC World we are definitely encouraged to be Scottish, Welsh, Irish or English first and British second. My bosses at the BBC have been banging on about the importance of recognising 'the nations' for as long as I can remember, and I think most of us have now had it dunned into our heads that it simply does not do to present the news as if you are addressing only people who live inside the M25. But a Pakistani friend at the BBC complained vociferously to me that this new nationalist trend was depriving her of a sense of identity which she had worked very hard to acquire; with a family in Pakistan, a childhood home in Birmingham and a married home in west London, she was, she said, perfectly happy to define herself as a British Pakistani – she was, apart from anything else, very proud to work for the British Broadcasting Corporation, an institution which meant a great deal to her relatives in Pakistan. But she could see no sense whatever in which she was 'English'. So just as she settles into the comfort zone of a new sense of home, the PC planning officials have come along to tell her that the place where she has pitched her tent does not really exist any more.

Anthony Browne, in the book I have discussed in the previous chapter, identifies the rise of Political Correctness with that of New Labour. 'In 1997,' he writes,

'Britain began, in effect, to be ruled by political correctness for the first time. The Labour government was the first UK government not to stand up to political correctness, but to try and enact its dictates when they are not too electorally unpopular or seriously mugged by reality, and even sometimes when they are.' Even if he is half right there is a certain irony in the fact that one of the most serious PC conflicts of twenty-first-century Britain erupted in the last months of Tony Blair's tenancy at Number 10.

Like many of the best rows, the dispute between the government and the Roman Catholic Church over adoption by gay couples began as an innocent-looking cloud on a distant horizon. The Equality Act – which prohibited discrimination in the provision of goods and services on the grounds of sexual orientation – passed into law without much fuss in 2006; it was designed to stop hotels turning away gay couples who want to share a room, or restaurants throwing them out for holding hands during a romantic dinner. I think we did have one cross Christian B&B owner on the *Today* programme complaining about being forced into complicity with immoral practices (if the way I have phrased that makes it sound as if he was being forced to join in, my apologies to him), but there was no great groundswell of public outrage about this relatively modest objective.

But in early 2007 the government tried to implement the Act through what were called the 'Equality Act (Sexual

Orientation) Regulations', which stated, to use the appropriately legal language, that 'where a religious organisation
provides services to the community on a commercial basis
or on behalf of and under contract with a public
authority', it must comply with the principles of non-
discrimination – and that meant that the adoption agencies
run by the Catholic Church would have to consider gay
couples as potential adoptive parents. The agencies in
question are generally acknowledged to be extremely
good, their cases account for only around 4 per cent of
the adoptions in Britain, and it is difficult to imagine a
gay couple who are planning to adopt going first to a
Catholic agency anyway – so one might have thought it
was in everyone's interest to find a practical solution to
the problem. The Equality Act does in fact include some
exemptions which could have offered a model; for
example, it allows a parish priest to retain the right to
decide who rents church premises, so Father Pro-life
will not have to let the church hall out for a meeting of
the local branch of Marie Stopes.

But it very quickly became apparent that this was an
argument about principle rather than practicalities. The
leaders of the Anglican Church weighed in behind their
Catholic colleagues with a letter to the Prime Minister,
which, despite its slightly mealy-mouthed, vicarish
language, drilled down to the meat of the matter. 'In
legislating to protect and promote the rights of particular
groups,' wrote Archbishops Rowan Williams of Canterbury

and John Sentamu of York, 'the government is faced with the delicate but important challenge of not thereby creating the conditions within which others feel their rights have been ignored or sacrificed, or in which the dictates of personal conscience are put at risk.' This was a clash of rights; on this rather unlikely battleground of a successful but relatively modest church social programme, the right to freedom of religion and the right to protection from discrimination went head to head. When the Catholic Church did agree to a compromise proposal – which would have involved signing up to a 'duty to refer' gay couples to other agencies – the Cabinet rejected it, greatly adding to the Catholic sense of grievance and the suspicion at the top of the church hierarchy that the dispute was indeed, in the words of one senior Catholic figure, about a 'politically correct agenda' rather than anything else.

I cannot make up my own mind about which side was right in this argument. It does seem batty that the Church should be confronted with a choice between compromising its principles and withdrawing from an important area of social action where it makes a valuable contribution. On the other hand, if we, through Parliament, decide that anti-discrimination policy is a priority, then surely it should apply to everyone, including big institutions like the Catholic Church, and especially so when they take public money – and the Catholic adoption agencies are funded by local authorities.

But I am sure that it is dangerous to leave one side in a dispute like this feeling that its rights have been violated in a fundamental way. The Catholic Church was given a couple of years' grace to work out how to adapt to the new regulations, but it was told that it would, in the end, have to abide by them. Cardinal Cormac Murphy-O'Connor, the Archbishop of Westminster, painted the outcome as a threat to that most basic of human rights, religious freedom. 'My fear is,' he said in a lecture delivered at the end of March 2007, 'that under the guise of legislating for what is said to be tolerance, we are legislating for intolerance.' The Cardinal's metaphors became somewhat tangled as he explored the implications of the decision, but his message was clear; he continued, 'My fear is that in an attempt to clear the public square of what are seen as unacceptable intrusions, we weaken the pillars on which that public square is erected, and we will discover that the pillars of pluralism may not survive . . . The question is whether the threads holding together pluralist democracy have begun to unravel.' And he put the incident into the context of a more general sense of alienation from British society: 'when Christians stand up for their beliefs, they are intolerant dogmatists. When they sin, they are hypocrites. When they take the side of the poor, they are soft-headed liberals. When they defend the family, they are right-wing reactionaries.'

The *Daily Mail*'s report of the speech suggested that Murphy-O'Connor was 'the first Catholic leader in nearly

180 years to put a question mark over the allegiance of his church to the British state', but it was not just the Catholics who felt bruised by the gay adoption episode; 'hear hears' could be heard from the heart of the British establishment, the Anglican benches in the House of Lords. At about the same time as the Cardinal's lecture the Right Reverend Michael Scott-Joynt, Bishop of Winchester, said, 'It looks to many of us as if at every point, where there is a serious tension between the human rights of different groups of people, and specifically the human rights of gay people – at every point gay rights trump everyone else's.'

The gay adoption row more or less coincided with a big change in the structure of our anti-discrimination quangos. Three organisations which had become all too familiar to PC warriors on both sides over the years – the Commission for Racial Equality, the Equal Opportunities Commission (which dealt with sexual discrimination) and the Disability Commission – were brought together under the banner of the Equalities and Human Rights Commission. The new body has the job of dealing with equality and discrimination in general, and that will mean adjudicating when there is a rights clash of the kind we saw in the row between the Catholic Church and government. The first boss of the organisation, Sir Trevor Phillips, has already shown himself sensitive to the risk of siding too readily with the politically correct view; he famously said that we were in danger of 'sleepwalking' into segregation and initiated an investigation into whether white families face discrimination in the allocation of council housing. But I do not envy him his task – even a cursory glance at his organisation's website reveals the potential for hideous hair-splitting of a kind that might defeat Solomon – and he is certainly likely to make the *Daily Mail* leader column on a regular basis.

The website's section on religious discrimination states, for example, that 'For the purposes of the Equality Act 2006, belief is defined as including philosophical beliefs, such as humanism, which are considered to be similar to a religion. Other categories of beliefs, such as support for a political party, are not protected by the Equality Act.' An interesting distinction that; I wonder what it would have meant for that old stalwart of British by-elections the Natural Law Party, or means today for the Sikh Federation. What would the Christian Democrats of Germany or Italy make of it? What, come to that, would Islamic parties in Turkey or Algeria have to say on the matter?

The website uses examples to illustrate what may and what may not be judged to be discriminatory. Some of them cover familiar ground. Thus,

A chief executive introduces a 'no headwear' rule for all staff. This would put Sikh men who wear a turban and Jewish men who wear a kippah at a disadvantage. This is an example of indirect religious discrimination, and would need to be justified otherwise it may be unlawful.

But others open up whole new vistas of merriment for those disposed to be satirical about the ways of a PC World. Here are a couple:

A religious woman frequently refers to her colleagues as 'sinners' and warns them that they will go to hell if they do not convert to her religion. This is an example of religious harassment.

And

A man who is an atheist is targeted by his Christian colleague, who believes that she must try to convert him to her religion. She leaves religious texts on his desk and tries to engage him in conversations about Christianity. The man complains to his employer, who tells him to ignore her. This is an example of harassment from a colleague on grounds of no religious belief. The employer is also liable to legal action for failing to deal with the harassment.

'Yippee,' you may say, if you have had an especially bad case of the God Squad at work. What a woosy, I say. Would any of us really go to court over a couple of flyers for the Alpha course?

Telling a Brit that he or she has no sense of humour is (forgive the stereotyping) like being rude about the food at a French dinner party or telling an Italian she has no dress sense – about as insulting as you can get. Even the authors of government guidelines seem to know this; if you dig deep on the Equalities and Human Rights Commission website you will find a copy of the 'Guidance on new measures to outlaw discrimination on grounds of religion or belief in the provision of goods and services' published by the Community Affairs Department, and you can read this pre-emptive strike against all those jokes about 'Winterval' and the like: 'Part 2 [of the Equalities Act] has nothing in it to discourage a public authority from recognising Christmas by putting up Christmas trees or sending Christmas cards to stakeholders. Many public authorities choose, as a matter of good practice and respect to minority faith and belief communities within their area or among their users to recognise their festivals too' but 'Where action is taken specifically to give recognition to a minority community through celebration of its festivals, care may be needed to ensure that the festivals of the predominant religion of the local community, which is usually Christian, are not overlooked.'

It is not exactly the most ringing endorsement of the deep Christian roots of our society and that great outpouring of fellow feeling we like to associate with Christmas, but I did think it was interesting that those behind the Equality Act felt the point needed to be made.

And then I read this headline in the *Sun*: 'BID TO BAN CHRISTMAS – Festive Fun Upsets Migrants, Says

Labour Think-Tank'. To someone writing a book about a PC World, a headline like that is like, well, Christmas coming early. And it gave me the theme of my next chapter.

# 5

# Pleasure in a PC World

The past is a foreign country: they do things differently there.

L.P. Hartley, *The Go-Between*

It is one of the great opening lines of English fiction, and it immediately invites you into a world untrammelled by today's PC anxieties. The next paragraph discovers a diary of the year 1900 and a battered box of childhood memorabilia – sea-urchin shells, rusty magnets and stumps of sealing-wax – and you are seduced into a place under licence for the indulgence of sentimentality and nostalgia.

L.P. Hartley's painfully tender evocation of a late Victorian English summer in a grand country house includes a pivotal description of the annual cricket match between 'the Big House' and the village. It has stuck in my mind because I once encountered the passage which follows in a Practical Criticism paper at university – and when you meet a piece of good poetry or prose under the intensity of exam conditions it burns itself into your consciousness. The narrator, for those who have not read the book, is a ten-year-old boy, the 'Go-Between' of the title. Sent to spend the summer with a school friend in a grandee's country home in Norfolk, he finds himself being used as a messenger in a love triangle; a neighbouring farmer, Ted, and a visiting aristocrat, Lord Trimingham, are competing for the affections of the grandee's daughter – and of course the outcome of the cricket match hangs on these two rivals in love.

Lord Trimingham sent down his deceptively dipping ball but Ted did not wait for it to drop, he ran out and hit it past cover point to the boundary. It was a glorious drive and the elation of it ran through me like an electric current. The spectators yelled and cheered, and suddenly the balance of my feelings went right over; it was their victory that I wanted now, not ours. I did not think of it in terms of the three runs that were needed; I seemed to hear it coming like the wind.

I could not tell whether the next ball was on the wicket or not, but it was pitched much further up and suddenly I saw Ted's face and body swinging round, and the ball, travelling towards me on a rising straight line like a cable stretched between us. Ted started to run and then stopped and stood watching me, wonder in his eyes and a wild disbelief.

I threw my hand above my head and the ball stuck there, but the impact knocked me over. When I scrambled up, still clutching the ball to me, as though it was a pain that had started in my heart, I heard the sweet sound of applause and saw the field breaking up and Lord Trimingham coming towards me. I can't remember what he said – my emotions were too overwhelming – but I remember his congratulations were the more precious because they were reserved and understated . . .

The passage, so precise in the way it captures the flame-like feelings of childhood and early adolescence, came to mind after a moment of pure pleasure which I experienced on a shoot in Devon a couple of years ago. I am extremely bad at shooting and I do it very seldom – once, perhaps twice a year at most, and very often not at all. But on this occasion I found myself hitting almost everything, and I shot more pheasants during the first drive than I usually do in a whole day. It may have been the beautiful gun lent to me by my host that worked the magic; it was one of a pair of Purdeys, a legacy from his father (a pair nowadays costs rather more than a small house in France), and the way it was balanced made you feel that those deadly, smooth black barrels would simply float through the swing and find their mark of their own accord.

For the third drive of the day the eight guns were ranged in a loose arc around a copse of silver birches which was, one of the keepers assured us, stiff with pheasants. Sure enough, the birds began coming with the first thwack of a beater's stick, and within a few minutes I had loosed off so many shells that I had run out of ammunition – I had to scamper humiliatingly over to my neighbour to plunder his cartridge bag. After that first flurry of killing there was a pause, three or four minutes to rest and take in the pale blue autumn sky and the soaked, violent green of West Country fields after rain.

Suddenly a single hen pheasant broke cover from the silver birches directly ahead of me, flying very high and very fast on the wind. As I raised my gun I was conscious that I was the only one with a bird in my sights – everyone else was watching me. The world seemed to slow down for a beat or two, and I pictured us – my hen and me – as we must have looked to our audience of beaters, keepers and the other guns; we were both moving very quickly in what felt like slow motion. I even had time to wonder whether she had looked down to see the polished stock and the silver chasing on the Purdey. As I pulled the trigger I sensed a line like the Go-Between's cable connecting me with my prey; the hen came down almost miraculously quickly, hitting the ground with the definitive thump of a cleanly shot bird. And, again like the Go-Between after his catch, I felt a glow of admiration emanating from my fellow sportsmen, and was childishly pleased by it.

It is very difficult to explain to those who do not shoot why shooting is a pleasurable pastime. Part of it, of course, is the scenery – and the compulsory communion with the elements involved in spending a cold (usually) day almost entirely outside. There is the camaraderie and the jollity; the breaks for hot sausages and slugs of Bull Shot or Bloody Mary, and the boozy, hearty lunches in converted barns and country pubs. There is also the licence for straight-laced men to indulge the English passion for dressing up; city bankers and lawyers whose usual uniform is a sober suit will spend huge amounts on garish tweed plus-fours, brightly coloured garters and beautifully polished leather accessories. There is the fun of watching well-trained dogs on their high-speed snuffles through the undergrowth as they search for dead or wounded birds. And part of the appeal is certainly a boyish competitive spirit.

But there is also the killing. Would I have enjoyed that moment of connection with my target as much if it had been a clay pigeon and not a beautiful bird? I do not think I would, if I am honest with myself. Anyone who enjoys blood sports has to admit that part of the fun is . . . well, the blood, really.

This is an unpleasant reality to confront, and we create rituals to rationalise it. If you go shooting you will, at the end of the day's sport, be given a brace or two of pheasants to take home. It is very unlikely that they will be the pheasants you have shot yourself (if you are as inaccurate as I usually am the odds against that are very high indeed), and some shoots will give you birds from a previous outing that have already been plucked, drawn and frozen for your convenience. But it preserves the fiction that you are killing to eat. By such small courtesies to our victims we acknowledge our awkwardness and ambivalence about killing for pleasure's sake alone.

The conservative commentator Paul Johnson – who is scarcely a natural ally of Political Correctness – recently wrote a powerful anti-shooting polemic in the *Spectator*. It included this vignette – which comes, as it happens, from roughly the same period where L.P. Hartley found his 'foreign country' of the past.

The Duke of Windsor describes an apocalyptic day before the first world war at Hall Barn, the estate near Beaconsfield belonging to Lord Burnham, owner of the *Daily Telegraph*. There a special show was put on to delight the King and his heir and five other expert 'guns'. Each used three weapons, thrust at them in turn by their 'handlers'. The King shot in a peculiar way, his left arm extended straight along the barrel, with both eyes open. The shooting started at 10 a.m., and continued for six solid hours, with a break for a sumptuous lunch in a big tent set up near the killing grounds. Up to 100 beaters drove the pheasants into the gun-stands, many of the birds having been specially imported so that the day could go down as the greatest shoot in history. The King, said his son, was 'deadly that day', and was seen to bring down 39 pheasants in succession, without wasting 'a single shot'. Altogether, he killed over 1,000 birds himself, out of a total of nearly 4,000 slain in those fatal six hours. The beautiful dead birds were laid out in rows of 100 each, the shooters bruised with the recoils, deafened by the noise. Even King George admitted at the end, 'Perhaps we went a little too far today.'

What, Paul Johnson asks, did the King mean by this 'cryptic confession'? Presumably that even hardened addicts are repelled when killing turns to slaughter.

If I spend too much time reflecting in this vein I find myself being drawn down a PC road I really do not want to travel. Not long after arriving at the boarding school I attended from the age of thirteen I was involved in a brutal ritual. My house, St Hugh's, shared a building on top of a small hill at the head of our North Yorkshire valley, and the slightly scruffy woods which skirted its slopes were full of rabbits. One Saturday we first-year boys were given hockey sticks and told to beat our way through the trees, sending the rabbits up towards the sixth-formers who had ranged themselves around the lawns. They too had hockey sticks, and as the terrified rabbits shot out of the woods they tried to knock their heads off. There was no reason for this killing fest – beyond the pleasure to be had from the act of killing. The older boys certainly did not eat or skin their bag of headless rabbits. My thirteen-year-old friends and I thought this was barbaric, and vowed that we would not continue the practice when we reached the dizzy heights of the sixth form ourselves – and we kept to that. If today someone was to make the case that killing pheasants in a Devon field was morally equivalent to the brutality of those sixth-formers, could I really answer the charge in a satisfactory way?

Moral logic says I should not mind the steady march of PC progress in circumscribing our pleasures. If shooting for sport is one day banned by those its enthusiasts would, I am sure, call 'the PC Brigade', could I claim that represented a fundamental infringement of our liberties? I am not sure that I could, especially not in a world where so many people are still not free to speak, worship or vote as they want.

But I cannot deny that it would sadden me greatly, and when I think of the pleasures that make my life rich, all too many of them involve a measure of cruelty.

I am, for example, an unreconstructed enthusiast for *foie gras*, and when, in October 2007 I read that York City Council had banned its sale on council premises I found myself harrumphing like the grumpiest anti-PC malcontent. There are very few tastes which can equal this glorious food, especially when it is taken with a golden glass of Montbazillac, ideally on a long summer evening in the Dordogne. There have been attempts to produce the delicious substance without cruelty, but I remain unconvinced. The *Daily Telegraph* offered a clever leader column on the subject:

A new delicacy is about to arrive in upmarket food halls: 'ethical' *foie gras*, produced by encouraging geese to gorge themselves for their own accord rather than force-feeding them. On the

Spanish farm where this technique was invented, geese wander around stuffing their faces until their bellies touch the ground. When their livers are big enough, they are then gassed to sleep and killed 'respectfully'. In other words we are forcing them to become clinically obese by surrounding them with figs and lupins (in the goose world, the equivalent of double cheeseburgers and chips).

Is that ethical? We are not sure – but what fun to be a fly on the wall at the first Islington dinner party at which a hostess serves 'ethical' *foie gras*.

I also have a passion for oysters, which I learnt to love during my posting as the BBC's correspondent in Paris. Walking home from the metro after a long day's broadcasting on one of those dank December days that make you wonder why anyone thought to call Paris 'the City of Light', I would sometimes stop at the supermarket and buy an enormous bag of *fines de claires*. Half an hour's shucking and stuffing at the kitchen table immediately restored my good humour. I know that the consciousness of these molluscs is less than Proustian, but from time to time I cannot help wondering how they experience a death which in human terms is not unlike being hanged, drawn and quartered – and I am perfectly sure that one of the reasons oysters offer that unique jolt of taste and sensation is that they are so close to being alive when you eat them.

France has declared *foie gras* to be 'part of the cultural

and gastronomic patrimony' of the nation, and therefore deserving of special protection, and the French shop-keepers who sold me my *fines de claires* would regard my occasional scruples about oyster-eating as an eccen-tricity bordering on madness. It is no accident that so many wicked pleasures originate in France; the French remain startling out of sympathy with the mores of a PC World.

François Mitterrand was president of France during my time as Paris correspondent, and I find him an endur-ingly fascinating figure because he embodies so many of our stereotypes about post-war French politicians and the French in general. In terms of sheer cleverness he was well beyond the reach of any leader that modern Britain has produced, but he was also bleakly cynical and irre-deemably amoral. And he was, of course, the least PC leader of the Left it is possible to imagine – the way he accumulated mistresses was almost casual, and his dedi-cation to sensual gastronomic experience was heroic. It is said that during his final days he indulged – as a kind of gastronomic Last Supper – in the exotic dish known as *ortolans*.

These tiny songbirds are pretty little things, with greenish heads, yellow throats and brown and black striped backs. They must be captured alive and then left for a month to gorge themselves on grapes and figs in a dark box (some connoisseurs prefer to blind them altogether); once they have swollen themselves to a grotesque size they are drowned in Armagnac, roasted and eaten whole, bones, feathers and all. Tradition dictates that the diners should cover their heads with huge, embroidered white cloths while indulging – some hold that this is to hide their cruel gluttony from God, others that it is to intensify the unique aroma of the bird, still others that it is simply a sensible precaution because of the monstrously repulsive practicalities of stuffing a grossly overweight roasted feathered creature into your mouth.

The delicacy is served so hot that it must be held on the tongue for a while, and one novice described his virgin *ortolan* experience like this:

the first taste was delicious, salty and savoury, swiftly followed by the delicate, incomparable flavour of the fat . . . By now it had cooled sufficiently to allow me to get the whole thing into my mouth. It was awkward, but not the struggle I had imagined. I was aware of fine bones but resisted the urge to crunch them immediately . . . Still sucking fat, I was aware of the richer, gamier flavour of its innards. I had been dreading this but the flavour remained delicate. Crunching the bones was like munching sardines or hazelnuts. I chewed a long time. When I finally had to swallow, I regretted the end of a very sensual experience.

The hunting of *ortolans* has long been banned in France (they are an endangered species) but it was not until the spring of 2007 that the French government declared that it was determined to enforce the law in this regard. The move provoked some controversy in France – especially in the south, where the birds are most commonly found. In the course of an interview with the *Daily Telegraph* on the subject, the restaurant critic of the French broadsheet *Le Figaro* alluded to what must surely be considered a *recherché* dispute, even by the peculiar standards of the gourmet. 'The bird is about the size of a young girl's fist,' he reported from the front line of *ortolan* eating. 'Some people begin with the head, others start with the rear end – there are competing opinions on how best to enjoy them.'

I love foods that make many other people go 'yuck', but I think an invitation to don the white tablecloth for a clandestine snack of songbird would be too much even for me, and the question of whether they are best enjoyed head or bum first is one I shall never try to settle. At the same time I greatly admire the fundamental honesty about the pursuit of pleasure which is characteristic of the French attitude to food; not for them the squeamishness of the Anglo-Saxon who shies away from the painful real-ities of eating other animals. The quintessential French food is that steaming pile of offal known as *Andouillette*. Anyone who has encountered this delicious dish knows that it smells, powerfully and unmistakably, of shit. This is because it is made from the colon of a pig, where, in the normal course of events, shit would be found. It is carefully cleaned before it is cooked, and no actual shit remains, but the relationship between the source of this pleasure – a pig's shit tube – and the aroma which makes it so magical is truly authentic. And, lest there be any doubt on this point, the dish is enjoyed precisely *because* of its shit-like smell, not despite it. When you eat *Andouillette* you do not try to forget where it has come from, you revel in it.

There is a similar frankness in the French attitude to sex. The English novelist Lucy Wadham has drawn the following conclusion from many years living in Paris:

It has become clear to me that the driving force behind sex in France is, quite simply, the pursuit of pleasure. Not ecstasy, not oblivion, but pleasure . . . There has always been a tendency in Britain to see sex without love as dirty. In the minds of the French middle classes, sex, even where love is absent, is a source of pleasure to which every human being has an inalienable right.

Her visits to her gynaecologist have, she reports, always ended with an inquiry about her own sex life; he 'would look up from his notes and with an earnest expression ask me *"Et le libido? Ca va?"* ', recommending a course of testosterone if she admitted to a falling off of desire. She has a wonderful anecdote about a friend's appointment with a GP which will strike a chord with anyone who has had one of those 'Lost in Translation' moments which remind the visitor to France that they are in a foreign country where 'they do things differently':

In the middle of the consultation there was a knock on the door. The doctor's secretary begged to be excused for an interruption. She had a patient on the phone who was complaining that she hadn't had an orgasm for a month and she wondered if it could be the result of the medication the doctor had prescribed. My friend watched the doctor in disbelief as he pondered the matter for a moment:

'*Non, non.* It's not the medication. It is probably psychological factors. Tell her she can make an appointment to discuss it.'

The secretary smiled sweetly at my friend and then closed the door behind her. Without the slightest ripple of unease, the GP picked up where he had left off.

I asked Lucy Wadham whether she could recommend any significant contemporary French writing on the subject of Political Correctness; she replied that such a thing does not exist – for the simple reason that no one in France really understands the meaning of the phrase. 'They order,' as Laurence Sterne's traveller remarks at the beginning of his pleasure-loving *Sentimental Journey*, 'this matter better in France.'

Sex and food are of course the routine clichés of writing about the French, but evidence of a non-PC view of the world pops up in every area of France's national life.

Covering the French presidential elections of 2007, I was struck by the way Jean-Marie Le Pen tried to smear Nicolas Sarkozy because of his central-European roots. In Britain we have adopted what are called 'dog whistle' politics. If you want to send out a nasty message you do it by saying something that seems perfectly acceptable but actually communicates your sympathy with an unpleasant but popular prejudice (usually having to do with foreigners); you hope that the point is taken by the intended audience because they are attuned to the hidden message in the way a dog is attuned to his whistle. Jean-Marie Le Pen did not bother with such PC sensitivities; he came straight out with it, accusing Mr Sarkozy of coming 'from an immigrant background' and declaring himself to be a candidate *du terroir* – a phrase which conjures up that sense of sacred soil which is so central to French culture.

Sarkozy is no slouch in these matters himself, having famously referred to the rioters who wrecked great swathes of France's suburbs in 2005 as *racaille* or 'scum' which needed to be hosed off the streets – an un-PC moment which might have ruined a political career in this country but in France proved no impediment to securing the keys to the Élysée Palace. And this kind of frankness is not confined to the French Right; when Ségolène Royal put herself forward as the Socialist Party's candidate for the presidency, Laurent Fabius, a former socialist prime minister, is reported to have asked, 'Who will look after the children?'

Because I took up my job in France immediately after three years spent living in the United States, the contrast between the French and American attitudes to Political Correctness was brought home to me especially vividly. My first real lessons in PC behaviour were taught to me by my producer–researcher in the ITN Washington bureau; if I made an inappropriate comment about, say, Fawn Hall (the implausibly gorgeous secretary at the centre of the Iran–Contra scandal) Marie would politely (because she was very well-mannered) but firmly reprimand me. By the time I left the United States for a job with the BBC in Paris I was well schooled. Brigitte, my researcher in the BBC Paris bureau, took a rather different view of such matters. Not long after arriving I did a report for *Newsnight* about the state of the French film industry, and in the course of it we interviewed the actress Mathilda May. The experience of talking to this surpassingly beautiful young woman had the regrettable effect of making me forget PC proprieties, and I am ashamed to record that over a drink with my producer – another male Brit – I discussed our interviewee in terms which Marie would have found most offensive. Brigitte overheard this conversation, and far from taking offence she thoughtfully cut out some magazine pictures of Ms May dressed only in lingerie and pinned them above my desk. She thought to please but I was, needless to say, both astonished and mortified.

In an essay about French attitudes to Political

Correctness written in the mid 1990s, the author Lisa Appignanesi, then living in Paris, recorded some of the factors cited by her French friends as reasons that PC would never take root in France. French is a gendered language, so the sort of 'politically correct manipulation' which I have discussed in Chapter 2 can seem somewhat pointless; 'Politics, beauty, truth, the republic,' Appignanesi points out, 'are already feminine words.' She also refers to 'the lack of cultural puritanism' in France, and although she gives puritanism a small 'p', comparisons between Political Correctness and the dour religion which sent the Pilgrim Fathers to Plymouth Rock are something of a leitmotif of writing on this subject. I have quoted earlier Stuart Hall's comments on the similarities between what he calls 'PC-ers' and 'latter-day saints like the Puritans of the seventeenth century' with their 'strong strain of moral self-righteousness'. Aidan Rankin, in *The Politics of the Forked Tongue*, writes of PC campaigners that 'as with the Puritans of old, they doubt the capacity of individuals to form opinions for themselves and, for all their talk of diversity, flatly refuse to accept the idea of "different strokes for different folks"'. And I picked up a hint of the po-faced Puritan world view when my fourteen-year-old step-daughter recently apologised for expressing an opinion which was not 'politically correct'; I asked her what she understood the phrase to mean, and she replied, 'It is what you are meant to think.'

France is – despite its Huguenot and secularist aberrations – a Catholic culture at heart; the United States has a strong dash of Puritanism in its national genes. Since the two countries represent opposite ends of the PC spectrum it seems reasonable to speculate that there may be a link between Political Correctness and religious culture. Catholic cultures tend to have a more relaxed attitude to rule-breaking, perhaps because of the tradition of the confessional; the Catholic Church sets very tough norms for what you should or should not do, but it has always operated on the assumption that you will often fail to meet them, and the Sacrament of Confession offers a ready and immediate possibility of forgiveness. Catholicism is also – since I am making generalisations here they might as well be broad – more at ease with the reality of those grand themes (Death, Glory, Sex, Sin, Eternal Life and the like) which are the natural currency of religion. That is reflected in Catholic aesthetics; those ghoulish bits and pieces of human remains you find preserved and honoured as saintly relics in southern European churches are the spiritual equivalent of *Andouillette*, their very ghoulishness – as authentic as the shitty smell of the dish – a reflection of the Catholic idea of the numinous, the routine interchange between the spiritual and material worlds. And above all, Catholic cultures are comfortable with the idea that religion (and therefore life) can be fun, whether it is expressed in the colour and movement of a Mardi Gras parade in Latin

America, the ridiculous architectural extravagances of a baroque church in southern Germany or the camp fastidiousness of a grand clerical outfitter's in Rome.

Like all elegantly simple antitheses this one – Catholic non-PC France versus Protestant PC USA – has an intriguing wrinkle. In Chapter 1 I briefly explored Paul Berman's idea that the intellectual godfathers of the PC World are the structuralist and post-structuralist philosophers, men like Jacques Derrida, Michel Foucault and Jacques Lacan. These figures are all, inescapably, French, and if I am right about the religious roots of PC and un-PC cultures they ought to be intellectual warriors on the other side. But Berman has a clever account of the journey that brought PC ideas from Left Bank cafés to the university campuses of the United States. They began, he argues, in the intellectual climate of 1968 and the French movement of that year known as *Les Evenements*. But they took a little time to cross the Atlantic, not least because not many American academics understand French. This piece of intellectual snobbery is, I hasten to add, his (and he is American) and not mine:

Radical leftism in the American sixties naturally made all kinds of efforts to work up some ambitious theories [he writes], and part of those efforts . . . was to import ideas from France. But that was slow going, possibly because the original works in French were translated only gradually, and in several cases made it into print only after the radical spark from the sixties was gone. Or it was because the French ideas were too baroque for American tastes, or too cynical . . .

French ideas, Berman argues, established themselves in American academia 'in waves of fashion . . . during the seventies and into the early eighties'. And during this transition period they acquired – this is more my gloss than Paul Berman's – a strong tinge of old-school American Puritanism. Certainly, the structuralist American academic trends which gave the anti-PC warriors of the late 1980s and early 1990s so much scope for satire were puritanical (with a small 'p') in the sense that they seemed designed to eradicate any idea that the arts can be regarded as a source of pleasure. Books and paintings became things which must not be enjoyed for themselves, but analysed only for what they can tell us about the social, political and economic conditions in which they were written and painted. The question of what works of art 'mean' has of course always been central to the study of literature or the visual arts as academic disciplines, and quite right too; but some of the critical writing of this period in America was uniquely reduc-tionist in the way it restricted its compass to a dourly intellectual exercise.

The jolliest attack on the structuralist school of criti-cism – and writing a funny book about structuralism is no small achievement – is Roger Kimball's *The Rape of the Masters – How Political Correctness Sabotages Art,* which was published in 2004. Kimball sets out to satirise the tendency to see art as 'a political intervention' rather than something which has intrinsic value. He makes his case by selecting seven famous paintings and quoting – at some length – some of the modern academic writing they have inspired.

My favourite is his essay on John Singer Sargent's *fin de siècle* masterpiece *The Daughters of Edward Darley Boit*, painted in Paris in 1882. The four children of this cultivated Bostonian exile are painted in an informal grouping in the family's apartment on the Avenue de Friedland. The picture is not portraiture in the conventional sense; the eldest of the girls, who is leaning with her back against one of a pair of vast Chinese pots, has a face largely lost in shadow. But it is at once satisfying and intriguing, pleasurable in itself and at the same time replete with a sense of untold stories – the sort of picture, in fact, that would make you want to linger if you encountered it in a gallery.

Kimball has dug out a book by a certain David Lubin, the Charlotte C. Weber Professor of Art at Wake Forest University, which argues that the picture is in fact all about – you guessed it – sex. Thus this passage on the doll which the youngest of the sisters – a four-year-old called Julia – is holding in her lap as she sits on the edge of an opulent-looking oriental rug in the foreground:

It forms a sort of buffer zone, that obstructs both the head-on gaze of the viewer and the direct approach of light from the painting's lower left corner. What this buffer zone protectively blocks from our gaze and from the revealing light is J's pudendum, as though to disclaim it, deny it, forswear its existence. J may thus . . . be characterised as thoroughly presexual and wholly unavailable to sexual investigation, whether scientific, artistic, or prurient. Nevertheless, that she protects her genital zone reflects how deeply sexualized she is, or how effective an act of repression this painting . . . must achieve in order to abide by an ideology of sexual innocence.

The real fun comes with the professorial riff inspired by the similarity between the Bostonian surname Boit and the French word for a box, *boîte*. 'Another way of accounting for the overall emptiness or lack that the painting bespeaks,' Professor Lubin suggests, 'is that the Female Child enclosed within this geometric and ideological box is also trapped within a biological box: the lack of the father's E, his penis.' You may want to re-read that sentence to make sure you have understood it, but since that 'E' is the first letter of the Christian name I share with the father of these enchanting little girls, I hurried on to find out more about its penis-like qualities – and was even more intrigued when I discovered that the little 'e' of *boîte* represents the clitoris:

What are the differences between big E and little e? To start, one is 'big' and the other 'little'. One is all hard right angles, straight and erect, while the other contains no straight angles but instead is softly curvilinear. One outwardly projects its elements . . . the other tucks itself inward; is, yes, womblike. (Or, if one prefers, clitoral . . .

At this point we are clearly a long way from the elegant Parisian salon so wonderfully evoked by John Singer Sargent, but we have further still to go. I shall let Roger Kimball take up the story here, because he does it so well:

Professor Lubin has a lot more to say about the Boit/Boîte connection. The one bit I feel I must share is his fugue on the circumflex over the letter 'i'. In French, as Professor Lubin notes, a circumflex denotes the fact that the letter 's' had at one time been part of the word in question. For Professor Lubin, that it is a deeply titillating fact.

'The circumflexed [this is now Lubin writing] *i* of boîte marks the absence of an *s*, the letter in the alphabet that not only commences the word sperm, but also resembles the sperm cell, the spermatozoon . . . One of the roles of the letter *s* is to make a singular word plural; thus not unlike sperm, *s* can have a reproductive function.

'The circumflex, inasmuch as it elides letters, makes words into contractions – a term that, outside the realm of grammar, has its own special place in the lingo of childbirth. Indeed, the circumflex, as typographical marking, can be seen in its own right as sexual, though now in a distinctly feminine, maternal way; as a sheltering tent; a bosom; a receptacle into which the central letter of boîte, the *i*, is phallically plunged . . . In the word boîte, the letter *i* has lost its rounded head in exchange for a spearhead; now it bears resemblance to an erect male member, the circumflexion producing the look of circumcision.'

'Clearly,' Kimball observes, 'Professor Lubin is not the sort of chap you want to leave alone with an underage circumflex.' I could not help thinking of the Professor's baroque, over-intellectualised and, in the end, frankly rather disgusting absurdity when, during an interview on the *Today* programme, the sculptor Sir Anthony Caro gave me the following simple and luminous answer when I asked him for his definition of art. 'We look at art first and foremost,' he said, 'because it delights us – it delights our eyes. So pleasure is a big part of it.'

And where are we, the British, in this exciting transatlantic swirl of religious contrast and cross-cultural fertilisation? As it happens, our history offers a neat parallel between Puritanism and Political Correctness which tells us something about both the nature of the PC phenomenon and the British attitude towards it: both Puritans and PC-ers are notorious for hating Christmas. One of Oliver Cromwell's many claims to fame is that he was associated with the first serious campaign in England to abolish this great festival – and Christmas-denial is of course one of the chief crimes of which PC warriors stand accused in the Court of Tabloid Opinion today.

The Puritan MPs of the Long Parliament began their assault on Christmas even before the Civil War began; in an early example of the PC approach to language they renamed it 'Christ-tide' to eliminate its residual connection with Roman Catholic mass, and in 1644 they tried to insist that 25 December should be kept as a day of fasting and repentance for the sins of those who had marked past Christmases by 'giving liberty to carnal and sensual delights'. In June 1647 they formally abolished the three great Christian feasts of Christmas, Easter and Whitsun, and more and more regulations were introduced over the next decade to reinforce the ban. There were fines for those found attending special Christmas services, and markets and shops were ordered to stay open for business on 25 December. In London soldiers were sent forth to sniff for the smell of a goose being cooked or any other tell-tale signs of seasonal cheer.

All this was accompanied by a more general, religiously inspired clamp-down on fun. Parliament considered a bill to stop women wearing make-up or immodest dresses, and the Puritan disdain for female vanity was enforced by Taliban-like troops who would stop women with painted faces and scrub them in the street. There was a New-Labourish campaign against binge-drinking. Several horse-races were prohibited, allegedly on grounds of national security. There was a scale for the punishment of swearing which varied by social degree (so that a duke paid thirty shillings, a gentleman only six shillings and eight pennies) and, as one writer on the period has put it 'The Assize Courts and Quarter Sessions . . . interested themselves in fornication.' Towards the end of Cromwell's rule the diarist John Evelyn noted that 'The religion of England is preaching and sitting still on Sundays.'

But in the end it did not really work. Popular enthusiasm for Christmas remained strong, and the general nostalgia for lost pleasures is reflected in a ballad called 'The World Turned Upside Down', which is preserved in the extraordinary collection of mid-seventeenth-century pamphlets and polemics known as the Thomason Tracts. Here are a few of its verses:

> Listen to me and you shall hear, news hath not been
> this thousand year:
> Since Herod, Caesar, and many more, you never heard
> the like before.
> Holy-dayes are despis'd, new fashions are devis'd.
> Old Christmas is kickt out of Town.
> *Yet let's be content, and the times lament, you see the*
> *world turn'd upside down.*
>
> . . .
>
> The serving men doe sit and whine, and thinke it long
> ere dinner time:
> The Butler's still out of the way, or else my Lady keeps
> the key,
> The poor old cook, in the larder doth look,
> Where is no goodnesse to be found,

*Yet let's be content, and the times lament, you see the*
*world turn'd upside down.*

To conclude, I'le tell you news that's right, Christmas
was kil'd at Naseby fight:
Charity was slain at that same time, Jack Tell troth too,
a friend of mine,
Likewise then did die, rost beef and shred pie,
Pig, Goose and Capon no quarter found.
*Yet let's be content, and the times lament, you see the*
*world turn'd upside down.*

In some towns attempts to enforce the anti-Christmas
ordinances led to riots, and when MPs met on 25
December 1656 – the day being, in the Parliament's eyes,
a working day like any other – many of them complained
that they had been kept awake at night by their neighbours preparing for a day of feasting, and that all the
capital's shops seemed to be defiantly shut. The
Restoration of the Monarchy in 1660 brought the restoration also of the full celebration of Christmas in its twelve
days' glory – to the general delight of the people. The
Puritan approach to Christmas did, however, live on a
little longer in the United States; the festival was banned
in Boston from 1656 until 1681, and the eating of mince
pies was forbidden in the city during the Christmas period.

The way this episode played out is a reflection of the
fact that we are – in this as in so many things – somewhere

between France and the United States. The British are as squeamish about extreme Puritanism as we are about unrestrained popery, and that is reflected in our conflicted attitude to the PC assault on Christmas today. Certainly you can hear echoes of those stern old Puritans in the annual crop of 'now they want to ban Christmas' stories which appear in the papers every year – the puritanical narrowness of vision and the lack of a sense of fun both inform some of the sillier expressions of Political Correctness which Christmas seems to inspire. But our national love of Christmas and its pleasures – both those that one might call religious, like singing carols, and those of the more material kind – is such that most of the noise comes from the defenders of tradition, and many of these stories are offered as satire, in the spirit of the seventeenth-century ballad I have just quoted, rather than as genuine news stories.

Some cracking examples of both kinds of Christmas story have – by coincidence – come my way during the writing of this chapter. My emails make a fizzing sound when they hit the inbox; I am sure I imagined this, but the one I received from Cristina Odone, former editor of the *Catholic Herald*, on 28 November 2007, seemed to have an especially indignant fizz when it arrived. She was 'incandescent' about the way she had been treated by the organisers of a carol service and wanted to share her feelings with the world (via the *Today* programme). The Royal Commonwealth Society had invited her to be one of the 'Celebrity Readers' at its annual carol service in the church of St Martin in the Fields. They asked her to write a short essay for the occasion on the theme of 'opportunities for all', and she was told that it could be 'political and controversial'; so she wrote a piece about secular intolerance towards religion. But she was informed that this would not do; 'I was told,' she said, 'that the words I had written were not appropriate because the congregation would include people of little or no faith who would presumably be upset. Even more insultingly, I was asked instead to read a passage from Bertrand Russell, a militant atheist.' Unsurprisingly, she pulled out of the event. The *Daily Telegraph*'s account of the story ended with this extremely enjoyable paragraph – the Mr Mole to which it refers was the director-general of the Royal Commonwealth Society: 'Mr Mole said he was "deeply sorry" Ms Odone felt unable to participate in the service but the tone of her script was too polemical for a "multi-faith" carol service.'

Eh? What's one of them then, when it's at home? You can do all sorts of things to a carol service; you can call it a concert and you can make it as 'inclusive' as you fancy, but you surely cannot entirely escape the fact that the excuse for all that hearty singing by candlelight is in some way connected with the (alleged, of course) birth of Christ.

And then there was that report from the Institute for Public Policy Research apparently suggesting Christmas should be 'ban[ned]' (if you read the *Sun*) or 'downgraded to help race relations' (if you read the *Daily Mail*). It attracted particular attention because the IPPR is – in a phrase we regularly use in *Today* programme scripts – 'New Labour's favourite think-tank', and Nick Pearce, who went on to be head of public policy at Downing Street, was the director of the IPPR at the time the report was commissioned. The passage that did the damage was this: 'Even-handedness dictates that we provide public recognition to minority cultures and traditions. If we are going to continue as a nation to mark Christmas – and it would be very hard to expunge it from our national life even if we wanted to – then public organisations should mark other religious festivals too.' That does not, of course, in fact suggest that Christmas should be abolished, and when I telephoned the IPPR they insisted that they had made no such proposal. But perhaps there is a certain puritanical wistfulness about the way the point is phrased; the conditional opening to the second sentence and that parenthetical reference to 'expunging' carry a Cromwellian hint of 'if only' about them.

By way of answer to the newspaper stories, the IPPR sent me a copy of their report; although I do not agree with many of its conclusions, it is a solid piece of work, and I shall return to it in the final chapter of this book. The Institute would not be the first to complain that their views on Christmas had been misrepresented. The annual lament about politically correct attempts to abolish this great festival is a hardy perennial of anti-PC journalism, and any newspaper stories appearing between mid November and early January which include the words 'Political Correctness gone mad' need to be treated with a great deal of caution. The *locus classicus* of the genre is the story that Birmingham City Council renamed Christmas 'Winterval'. There is a little bit of truth at the heart of the story: the council did indeed run a promotional campaign called Winterval – for a couple of years in the late 1990s – which was designed to attract business to the city centre. But in all other respects civic Birmingham continued to celebrate Christmas in the usual way – with lights in city-centre streets and trees in the big squares. The *Guardian* ran a piece trying to debunk the myths about Christmas in our PC World in December 2006, and the paper's reporter telephoned Birmingham City Council in the course of his researches; he reported meeting 'a silence that might seasonably be described as frosty'. A weary council spokesman told him, 'We get this every year . . . It just depends how many rogue journalists you get in any given year. We tell them it is bollocks, but it doesn't seem to make any difference.' And of course a moment's reflection will tell you that no city council has the power to 'ban' Christmas anyway; things have moved on a bit since the mid-seventeenth century.

The persistence of the Winterval urban myth is an instructive illustration of the power of the 'cuttings phenomenon'; once a story is out there and recorded in the news archives, it is more difficult than Dracula to kill.

In many cases this does not matter very much; it must be very tiresome to be that Birmingham City Council press officer taking those endless calls about a dodgy story a decade old, but the matter probably does not greatly trouble the people of England's second city as they go about their daily business. However, the way some of these stories are misreported dabbles in prejudice in a nasty way.

In December 2005 the *Express* ran a huge headline which declared that 'CHRISTMAS IS BANNED; IT OFFENDS MUSLIMS'. The lead paragraph of the story continued: 'Britain's proud heritage suffered a devastating blow yesterday after council chiefs banned Christmas. Critics accused a politically correct local authority of being ashamed to be Christian.' The rather modest 'fact' at the heart of this story was that advertisements for the switch-throwing ceremonies at street light displays in the London Borough of Lambeth referred to them as 'winter lights' and 'celebrity lights' rather than Christmas lights. It was, according to the *Express*, an 'astonishing diktat' by Lambeth Council.

Lambeth very quickly tried to kill the story. Decisions about what to call the lights in the advertisements had, a council spokesman said, been taken locally, not by the council. He complained that the council press office had received no call from the *Express* to check the accuracy of the story or ask for a comment, and added, 'Our response to the story was that it was absurd. Christmas was going on as usual. The Christmas tree was up in the Town Hall, the usual Christmas carols were being sung, the lights were up.' As a resident of the borough I am happy to report that we put up our Christmas tree as usual, stuck a Christmas wreath on the front door and were able to drive across the river to Westminster Cathedral for mass on Christmas Day without being stopped by the Gestapo.

Small ruckus in Lambeth, few dead, you might say. But the story was picked up by the authors of *The Search for Common Ground*, a report on the way Muslims are represented in the media which was commissioned by the then mayor of London, Ken Livingstone, and published in the autumn of 2007. Much of the material in this report was of dubious value (does it really mean very much to say that in a given week more than 90 per cent of stories about Islam in national papers were 'negative', for example?) and its conclusions certainly did not justify Ken Livingstone's claim that it amounted to a 'damning indictment' of the media. But on this particular story the authors had a point. 'There was,' they noted, 'nothing in the news item to substantiate the headline that Christmas offends Muslims, or even that anyone has ever thought that it offends Muslims.' Indeed, the body of the story actually carried a quote from the Muslim Council of Britain condemning Lambeth's alleged anti-Christmas bias.

That whopping headline 'CHRISTMAS IS BANNED;

IT OFFENDS MUSLIMS' is built on an entirely false premise; there are plenty of potential sources of tension between Muslims and non-Muslims in post-9/11 Britain, but Muslim objections to Christian festivals is not one of them. A few years ago I made a Radio Four documentary about the curious way in which the English remain attached to the idea of an Established Church and the web of archaic ties between Church and state that involves. We found that the most enthusiastic antidisestablishmentarianists were not crusty old Anglican bishops but rabbis and imams; they told us that the existence of an Established Church preserves a religious space in British society which has made it easier for new faiths to find a home here. The fact that this overwhelmingly secular country still celebrates a religious festival in such a very public way is, to most Muslims, a source of reassurance, not offence.

Stories of the 'Christmas is banned in a PC World' kind have become as seasonable as holly and mistletoe, but in December 2007 a couple of heavyweight political figures weighed into the conversation in a manner that gave it a more serious tone. The Conservative leader David Cameron picked up on the fact that some of these stories paint a false picture of minorities. 'The idea,' he said 'that anyone could ever be offended by a Christmas card that says "Merry Christmas and happy new year" and that we have got to send one saying "Season's greetings"; I think it's just insulting tosh. In fact people – Muslims and Jews

– are offended because it's treating them in a silly and politically correct way.' At the same time Sir Trevor Phillips, chairman of the new Equalities and Human Rights Commission which I discussed in the previous chapter, gave a 'pro-Christmas' speech in which he urged all schools to hold Nativity Plays.

There was a 'pro-pleasure' subtext to Sir Trevor's argument – he said children were missing out on something valuable if their schools chose not to keep up the Nativity Play tradition – but he too felt the usual crop of 'Christmas is banned' stories were doing real damage to good community relations by playing up the prejudice that non-Christian minorities are Christmas haters. 'A lot of these stories about Christmas are the usual silly season stuff,' he said. 'But I can't help feeling there's sometimes an underlying agenda to use this great holiday to fuel community tensions. That's why I asked leaders in different religious communities to join me in saying, "It's time to stop being daft about Christmas. It is fine to celebrate and it's fine for Christ to be the star of the show."' Pressed on the *Today* programme about who he had in mind when he made that accusation, he said – showing an unexpected tabloid flair – that some of those responsible were 'a small, misguided, rather grim group of nobby no-mates in public authorities', but he also blamed 'the "political-correctness-is-taking-us-to-hell-in-a-handcart-brigade" in some of our newspapers and some of our extremist parties'.

I assume that Sir Trevor was referring to the British

National Party there – and what a very depressing place that is to end a chapter that was supposed to be devoted to Pleasure. I have done my best to have fun in the PC World I have been exploring with the writing of this book, but I keep finding myself being drawn back to really quite tough questions about who we are, and how we think of ourselves.

# 6

# The past in a PC World

The wolf said, 'I am happy with *who* I am and *what* I am,' and leaped out of bed. He grabbed Red Riding Hood in his claws, intent on devouring her. Red Riding Hood screamed, not out of alarm at the wolf's apparent tendency to cross-dressing, but because of his wilful invasion of her personal space.

Her screams were heard by a passing woodcutter person (or log-fuel technician, as he preferred to be called). When he burst into the cottage he saw the melee and tried to intervene. But as he raised his axe, Red Riding Hood and the wolf both stopped.

'And just what do you think you're doing?' asked Red Riding Hood.

The woodcutter person blinked and tried to answer, but no words came to him.

'Bursting in here like a Neanderthal, trusting your weapon to do your thinking for you!' she exclaimed. 'Sexist! Speciesist! How dare you assume that womyn and wolves can't solve their own problems without a man's help!'

James Finn Garner, *Politically Correct Bedtime Stories*

W hile writing this book I have been forced to confront an extremely uncomfortable truth about my past: at the age of nineteen I was a repulsive little turd.

The conclusion was forced on me as a result of an email I received from a producer at Anglia Television. She had, she explained, found a copy of a 1977 item on the station's local news programme which featured an interview with me and some of my friends. Did I remember it, and might we all be willing to get together for a feature in a new series Anglia was running called *Where Are They Now?*

I did indeed remember the interview. It came about because a group of us – keen undergraduate journalists all – had been invited to contribute to a student edition of the humorous magazine *Punch*, which in those days was still something of a national institution. And when I got in touch with my old muckers – all of whom had since become distinguished figures in their various professions – they proved surprisingly sympathetic to the idea of a reunion.

At Anglia's invitation we gathered in a café in Westminster and watched our much younger selves performing; the interviewer's enormous kipper tie gave us much merriment, and we were surprised to find that in the 1970s we had such la-di-da accents that we all sounded like the Queen. Laughter and shared embarrassment melted any residual awkwardness there might have been about meeting after so long – some of us had stayed in close touch with one another, others had drifted into different worlds over the years – and soon old jokes and teases were being revived. It is surprising how quickly one reverts to childish behaviour when in the company of people one knew when one was very young.

It was, we all agreed, an entirely positive experience. Except for one thing: the programme-makers had tracked down a copy of our student edition of *Punch*, and one or two of us made the mistake of actually re-reading what we wrote all those years ago. I contributed two pieces to the magazine, one of which was a lament about the way university romance had been corrupted – as I apparently saw it – by the new fad for 'sexual politics' (which I wittily described as 'a curiously oxymoronic concept linking the most public and most private of Man's activities'). The piece is not even remotely funny, and it includes lots of arch, fogeyish comments about feminism and 'the campaign for homosexual rights'. Here is a flavour of the ghastly tone:

NAG, the Nursery Action Group, feels that the University Authorities should take care of the children they are so distressed to discover they can conceive. Most of its members wear two badges; one asks you to 'Scream for a Nursery', the other [declares] 'Abortion, a woman's right to choose'. They do not even have the decency to look coy when you point out the charmingly feminine illogicality of demanding a nursery when they are determined to have nothing to put in it.

Ouch, ouch and triple ouch. How and why did I come to imagine that that was amusing? I must, I suppose, have been confident that most of those who read it would have thought it clever in some way, and that I was playing to a view of feminism that was widely shared. I would surely not have written that if I had thought my student peers would have found it as offensive as I find it today, and there is a very obvious conclusion to be drawn from this embarrassing foray into the past: a more politically correct social and intellectual climate really would have made a difference.

It should be no great surprise that so many of the bitterest battles about Political Correctness have been fought on the fields of childhood and adolescence; the way today's young minds are formed will of course decide the social attitudes of the next generation. The Battle of the Books (which inspired the squib I have quoted at the beginning of this chapter) has been going for almost half a century – and long pre-dates the general use of the phrase 'Political Correctness'. The first recorded ban on the *Little Black Sambo* story was in 1956 (in Toronto); I can remember enjoying the tale of Sambo and the tigers who turned into butter as a child in the 1960s, but I was probably part of the last generation to do so before the racial crudeness of the book's illustrations made them so controversial.

Several decades later, in a new millennium, the same ground is still being contested. In 2007 Tintin, the intrepid journalist created by the Belgian cartoonist Hergé, came under fire for a similar reason. The book chain Borders was reported to the Commission for Racial Equality for selling copies of *Tintin in the Congo*; 'This book,' a spokes-woman for the CRE told *The Times*, 'contains images and words of hideous racial prejudice, where the "savage natives" look like monkeys and talk like imbeciles . . . How and why do Borders think it is okay to peddle such racist material?' Newspaper reports of the incident pointed out that Hergé had himself apologised for this particular episode in Tintin's adventures – using rather the kind of argument I might use to justify the youthful lapses I have admitted above. 'The fact is that while I was growing up I was being fed the prejudices of the bourgeois society that surrounded me,' he said. 'I portrayed these Africans according to ... the purely pater-nalistic spirit of the time.' He even recast some scenes in later editions; for example, the original has Tintin addressing a class of Africans thus: '*Mes chers amis, je vais vous parler aujourd'hui de votre patrie: la Belgique*' ('My dear friends, I am going to talk to you today about your fatherland: Belgium'). In the 1946 edition this scene was replaced by a mathematics lesson.

Not all authors are as willing to swim with the flow as Hergé apparently was. At about the time of the latest Tintin ruckus, the children's author Anthony Horowitz published a ferocious diatribe against the way his creative freedom was becoming constrained – he felt – in a PC World.

When it comes to children's literature [he wrote], the most fun a writer can have is creating the bad guys . . . and the fact is that there's nothing kids like more than a good villain . . . I have a hero in my books. His name is Alex Rider and I'm about to launch him on his seventh adventure, *Snakehead*. But I've found it increasingly difficult to create someone for him to fight: a bad guy who won't give offence, who won't break some new piece of politically correct legislation, who won't in short, damage my career.

Horowitz complained that he could not make his villain 'black, religious or homosexual', could not make him disabled ('unlike Captain Hook') could not make him fat ('When was the last time you saw Billy Bunter on the shelves?') and certainly could not make him a Muslim ('and even as I type that six letter word, I find myself a little nervous in case I'm misconstrued').

Politicians, of course, love this kind of thing and have been squabbling about it for years. In 1983, in a very early example of the power of anti-PC journalism, the *Daily Mail* reported that one of the schools run by the Inner London Education Authority (now defunct but at the time under Labour control) was offering a book called *Jenny Lives with Eric and Martin* in its library. It is a picture-book story – originally written in Danish – of a five-year-old girl being brought up by two gay men, and the good old-fashioned furore this news provoked led eventually to the passing of the famous (or infamous, depending where you stand) 'Section 28' amendment to the Local Government Act of 1988. This stated that local authorities should not 'intentionally promote homosexuality or publish material with the intention of promoting homosexuality' or 'promote the teaching in any maintained school of the acceptability of homosexuality as a pretended family relationship'.

For the Conservatives who introduced the measure it proved enduringly toxic. When the newly elected Labour government decided to repeal it at the end of the 1990s the Tories were badly split on the issue and it led to some high-profile defections. It gave the government problems too; successive defeats in the House of Lords prolonged the process of repeal, which was not achieved until 2003. And even that did not completely soothe the sensitivities that had been rubbed raw by *Jenny Lives with Eric and Martin.* In 2007 there was a pilot scheme to introduce a new set of reading books along the same lines – this time translated from the Dutch. *King and King* tells the story of a queen who wants her son to get married. 'She arranges for a string of princesses to meet him but he does not fall in love with any of them. In the end it is the brother of one of the princesses who catches his eye. The princes get married and become two kings.' *Spacegirl Pukes* is the story of a would-be child astronaut who falls sick and is nursed back to health by her parents, mummy Loula and mummy Neenee, and *And Tango Makes Three* tells of a pair of gay penguins in a New York zoo who are given an egg to hatch by an observant and sensitive keeper. Most of the objections this time came not from the Conservatives, who were now in their more forward-looking Cameron phase, but from religious groups, both Christian and Muslim. It is perhaps worth recording as a postscript that *Jenny Lives with Eric and Martin*, the book that began it all, appears to have acquired collectible cult status. When I tried to buy a copy I found three first editions of this slim volume on Amazon; they were selling for between £100 and £150 each.

Underlying all of these arguments is a deeper question about the purpose of education. In the summer of 2007 Civitas, the think-tank which produced the Anthony Browne pamphlet I have discussed earlier, launched a broader assault on the way Political Correctness has influenced the curriculum in general. *The Corruption of the Curriculum* is a collection of essays dedicated to making the case that

subjects in the school curriculum used to be regarded as discrete areas of knowledge, which would be imparted to pupils by teachers motivated by a love of learning. This has not been enough for recent governments, who see schools as a means of promoting social and political goals that may or may not relate

to traditional academic disciplines. This has given us geography
as a vehicle for environmentalism; history that neglects major
events and personalities; science classes in which pupils discuss
global warming without having the knowledge base on which to
make an informed judgement . . .

and so the list of corrupted subjects goes on. In his introduction to the book the sociologist Frank Furedi – a
long-standing critic of the ways of a PC World – argues
that 'the school curriculum has become estranged from
the challenge of educating children . . . issues that are
integral to education have become subordinate to the
imperative of social engineering and political expediency'. He is especially concerned about the way the
teaching of history is influenced by PC considerations,
and the theme is taken up in a chunky essay by Chris
McGovern, a headmaster and former Number 10 policy
adviser who, as the blurb reminds us, 'as a member of
the group that revised the National Curriculum for history
in the mid-1990s . . . published a critical minority report'.

McGovern cites one of those surveys – conducted by
the BBC, as it happens – which provide such enjoyably
shocking evidence of the ignorance of today's youth. Half
those aged 16–34 who took part did not know that the
Battle of Britain was fought during the Second World
War, and a third of them failed to spot the name of the
victor in the Battle of Hastings when asked to choose
between Napoleon, Wellington, Alexander the Great and

William the Conqueror. Quite a lot of them thought that Gandalf, Horatio Hornblower or Christopher Columbus was the hero of England's victory over the Spanish Armada. 'Does any of this matter?' McGovern asks rhetorically. His answer provides my theme for the remaining pages of this book:

Most surely it does. In fact, it matters profoundly – not for the sake of a good education for our children but also for the future stability and coherence of our multi-racial society. To know the history of one's country is a birthright. It tells us who we are and how we got here. It tells us how our shared values came into being. A people that does not know its history is a people suffering from memory loss, amnesia – a damaging illness.

In other words, the way we understand history is inseparable from the issue which has – in different guises – forced its way to the forefront in almost every chapter of this book: identity.

While I have been working on this project there has been a continuous and increasingly insistent hum of national conversation on this subject. It preoccupies everyone from the highest in the land – building a sense of Britishness has been close to an obsession for Gordon Brown – to the lowest, who vote for the British National Party. It underlies many of the anxieties of religious groups and minorities which I have discussed, and it is at the heart of most of the social projects I have described which are accused of 'Political Correctness gone mad' by their opponents. And if McGovern is right about the link between history and identity, then the way we understand history will dictate what our PC World becomes.

I am conscious that I am approaching this from the perspective of someone who, by accident of birth and education, grew up with a very strong sense of the past and a comfortable feeling about its relationship with my own identity. The Benedictines, who ran the school where I was educated, have, as they say, 'a good story to tell' about their own place in history, and it is a very long one. St Benedict was a Roman nobleman from the town of Nursia in what is now Perugia; he was born around 480 and the Rule he wrote to regulate the lives of his monks remains the heart of Benedictinism a millennium and a half later – so we boys were being educated according to an ethos with its roots in Imperial Rome. The Benedictine tradition of liberal education goes back many centuries, and we were taught that monasteries had played a decisive role in the survival of classical civilisation during Europe's dark ages, preserving and copying manuscripts in their scriptoria and libraries. The community which settled at Ampleforth in the early nineteenth century had spent the long years since the English Reformation in exile in France, so its traditions were cosmopolitan, but its location enhanced our sense of being part of a specifically English tradition too; that part of North Yorkshire is

littered with the ruins of the great religious houses which
dominated north-east England until the Dissolution of
the Monasteries.

All these things made it that much easier to make the
sort of connections which can bring a liberal education
alive. Latin, which I studied until A level and at eighteen
(though certainly not now) could read with something
close to fluency, did not really seem a dead language at
all; it was the natural language of monastic life and we
prayed in it on Sundays. So reading and enjoying one of
Horace's odes or a passage of Virgil did not feel like a
particularly peculiar or precious thing to do. The Prior
in the *Canterbury Tales* was not an exotic figure from
some distant and long-gone world; we had a prior of our
own (who, in a rather Chaucerian manner which gave
great pleasure to us and even more to the tabloid press,
fell in love with the mother of one of his pupils and left
the monastery). It was more natural to feel close to the
great events of European history because the monks who
taught us (or at least their spiritual antecedents) had been
around to see most of them. And, perhaps most importantly of all, we were conscious of the symbolic significance of the very existence of a Roman Catholic monastery
on English soil; it was a reminder of this country's long
national argument about religious identity, and living
evidence that the argument had, in most ways that
mattered, been resolved.

So at eighteen I emerged into the world with a sense

of cultural, religious and national identity which I now realise was almost unnaturally well developed and benign. I felt English, British, Catholic and part of the mainstream of European civilisation all at once. The Catholic bit lent a tiny seasoning of minority sensibility to the mix, but not in a way that compromised our self-confidence or involved any actual disadvantage. When I thought about the past, I thought about it as my own. I am afraid it made me smug – see the repulsive little turd episode above – but it was a remarkable privilege.

Just how remarkable a privilege I have only really come to appreciate since doing the research for this book. The case for a PC approach to history is very largely driven by the desire to create for everyone the kind of relationship with the past that I took for granted. Take, for example, *The Power of Belonging*, the pamphlet I quoted in the last chapter which prompted those outraged tabloid headlines about banning Christmas. It is PC to its syntactical fingertips (it refers, for example, to a 'sense of shared histories' rather than a singular history), but its arguments are all predicated on the idea that tradition has a profound impact on identity.

Thus it approvingly quotes Gordon Brown when he invoked one of our great national myths (I mean the word in a positive sense, not to imply that the story is a false one) to explain his vision of Britain: 'just as in war time a sense of common patriotic purpose inspired people to do what is necessary, so in peace time a strong modern sense of patriotism and patriotic purpose which binds people together can motivate and inspire'. And when the authors propose the idea of a new national holiday to help people reflect on the meaning of being British (a 'national civic day'), they turn to history for help:

And what about the date? The problem is that there is no single founding date of our nation state, and moreover, if it is to be genuinely British (rather than exclusive to one of the different nations within Britain) then we are restricted to commemorating an event that has occurred since the Act of Union in 1707. We believe that Armistice Day (or rather the Monday following Remembrance Sunday) would be the most appropriate. This builds on an existing commemoration rather than imposing something new and artificial.

A similar theme comes through an article that one of the authors of the pamphlet, Rick Muir, wrote to counter the press criticism over the 'abolish Christmas' carry-on; 'shared identity,' he wrote, 'should be built around our democratic values . . . These values are not abstract free-floating ideas, but are anchored in a long history and are embodied in our public institutions.' You might think that an appreciation of the power of history was a naturally conservative (with a small c) instinct; in a PC World it is well understood by those who want to make what this pamphlet calls the 'progressive case' for that old-fashioned-sounding idea of a 'national identity'.

That has had a surprising and almost paradoxical consequence; at just the time when those of the McGovern
school of thinking are beating their breasts over the woeful
ignorance of today's youth, the level of interest in history
and its meaning has become intense – much more so, I
suspect, than it was when I was studying it in the old-
fashioned way as a schoolboy in the 1970s. One of the
most passionate public rows of 2007, for example, was the
debate inspired by the 200th anniversary of the abolition
of the slave trade. I for one was taken aback by the extent
of support for the idea that Britain – in the person of its
queen or prime minister – should make a formal apology
for its role in the trade. John Sentamu, the Archbishop
of York and a church leader who has won himself real
moral authority, told Tony Blair that expressing 'deep
sorrow and regret' on behalf of Britain was not enough.
'Britain is our community and this community was involved
in a very, very terrible trade,' Dr Sentamu said. '. . . It is
really important that we own up to what was collectively
done. This is the moment in which you say "By the way,
I think our forebears did a terrible, terrible thing." ' Writing
in the *Guardian*, the black commentator Gary Younge
offered an imaginary version of the apology speech Mr
Blair might have delivered, and he cast the argument
explicitly in terms of the power of the past:

I apologise for our nation and our parliament. I offer the apology
unreservedly and unequivocally. I utter it with no lawyerly caveats

or tepid reservation. I am sorry. I say it not to pander to any particular community but because unless we can distinguish right from wrong in the past, there is little hope of us righting wrongs in the present.

My instincts were with those who said that apologising for something your ancestors did centuries ago is a cheap gesture which risks stripping the concept of 'apology' of any real meaning; it is easy to say you are sorry for a sin committed by someone long dead, and, rather like going into the confessional with your fingers crossed, I am not sure it has any real redemptive power. But looking back it seems to me that the debate was an extremely healthy one. Those arguing for an apology were using that as a way of reclaiming this piece of history as their own, and insisting that it be told in a way that acknowledges the perspective of the victims. Before the debate took place most Brits of my age probably thought of our country's past in relation to slavery in terms of its honourable record as the champion of abolition – rather than its shameful record as an enthusiastic slaving nation. One of the surprise publishing successes of 2007 was a whopping tome called *The Bumper Book of Look and Learn* – an anthology from the factual weekly comic that was such a familiar feature of school life in the 1960s and 1970s. I find leafing through it huge fun, partly because it is genuinely informative and partly because it immediately transports me back to the Britain of my youth, with all the cultural and social attitudes that implies. Here is *Look and Learn*'s take on the history of slavery which, it says,

developed on a large scale after the discovery of America at the end of the 15th century. The conquering Spaniards, finding themselves short of labour, decided to kidnap and transport into slavery Negroes from Africa.

In the next 60 years, the trade became so profitable that the Elizabethan sailor, Sir John Hawkins, took part in it with the Queen's approval.

But it was the cruellest and most inhumane act that one man could do to another. Why was it allowed? The Negroes were powerless to protect themselves. Why was there nobody who could save them?

One man made up his mind to try. His name was William Wilberforce, and he was a Yorkshire schoolboy when he first realised the full horror of the slave trade . . .

Did you notice how two centuries of British slaving simply disappeared in a paragraph break there? I suspect the public hubbub the subject generated in 2007 may have alerted many people of the *Look and Learn* generation to the weakness of that way of telling this chapter of our history. I have mentioned that I visited the slaving forts on the coast of Ghana as a teenager; during the *Today* programme discussions we had at the time of the abolition bicentenary, I often found the image of that hypocritical little white Anglican chapel above the slave dungeons swimming into

my mind. And perhaps I lost a little smugness as a consequence.

In the autumn of 2007 Trevor Phillips, the head of the
Equality and Human Rights Commission, tried a little
historical revisionism of this kind at a fringe meeting –
on, no great surprise, the subject of identity – during the
Labour Party Conference. Phillips quoted the theory that
an English alliance with the Ottoman Empire was a significant factor in the defeat of the Spanish Armada; Queen
Elizabeth's spymaster, Walsingham, apparently wrote to
his ambassador in Istanbul asking him to use 'all your
endeavour and industry' to persuade the Ottomans to
harass the Spanish in the Mediterranean and distract their
efforts from their English prey. The tactic worked – at
least so the argument goes – and that means that a Muslim
power played a significant part in this defining moment
of our Island Story, a perfect parable for a PC World if
ever there was one. The speech inspired a piece in the
*Observer* by the historian Tristram Hunt; he was rather
snooty about the evidence which formed the basis of the
Phillips claim, but he allowed that 'traditionalists have
objected to Phillips' call to "rewrite history" as a sinister
Left–liberal attempt to undermine national heritage with
multicultural fads. There are legitimate gripes about this
approach to history, but "rewriting the past" is not one
of them. Every generation and historian since Tacitus has
refashioned the past in the light of contemporary concerns
and personal foibles.' And that, of course, applies just as

much to historians of the Right as it does to those of the Left.

In fact, one of the pillars of the PC tradition of historical revisionism, a big fat piece of scholarship called *Black Athena*, is a prolonged exemplum of the idea that telling history is really an exercise in unravelling the ideas of people who have told it before. The author, Martin Bernal, is a scholar in modern Chinese political thought rather than the Classics, but the work for which he is famous is an assault on the notion that classical civilisation was a 'white culture'. His title is deliberately provocative; Athena was one of the greatest deities of ancient Greece and a central figure in defining the values we now associate with its culture; she was a daughter of Zeus, inventor of the plough and creator of the olive tree, a goddess in whom 'power and wisdom are harmoniously balanced', and above all the patron of Athens, the cradle of democracy. If it can be demonstrated that she was, in the sense we use the word today, 'black', that really would be a coup for the PC version of the past.

Bernal's argument is that ancient Greece was the creation of Africans and Arabs, the result of 'colonisation, around 1500 BC, by Egyptians and Phoenicians who had civilised the native inhabitants'. He says the ancient Greeks themselves understood that fact perfectly well and that 'Furthermore, Greeks continued to borrow heavily from Near Eastern cultures.' And he believes that this way of looking at classical civilisation survived right up until the middle of the eighteenth century, when it was challenged by the emergence of what we would now called racism in Western European thought. Wicked Christians and Romantics, he believes, put about the 'paradigm of "races" that were intrinsically unequal in physical and mental endowment' (no, I did not know that racism emerged from Romanticism either, but that is what the man says). They rewrote history to fit with the theory that 'To be creative, a civilisation needed to be "racially pure"', and reinvented ancient Greece as a white civilisation. Bernal breaks into editorialising italics to underline the importance of his theory:

*If I am right . . . it will be necessary not only to rethink the fundamental basis of 'Western Civilisation' but also to recognise the penetration of racism and 'continental chauvinism' into all our historiography, or philosophy of writing history . . . For 18th- and 19th-century Romantics and racists it was simply intolerable that Greece, which was seen not merely as the epitome of Europe but also as its pure childhood, [could] have been the result of the mixture of native Europeans and colonizing Africans and Semites.*

So this massive, lifetime's work – the first volume of *Black Athena* came out in 1987, the third was published in 2006 – is in fact a hugely ambitious project of cultural re-engineering. Bernal is mounting a PC challenge to the very basis of Europe's sense of its own identity.

There is, however, a small problem: almost all serious classical scholars think Bernal's central thesis is tosh.

It was a convivial evening at a Cambridge college in the company of Mary Beard, the Professor of Classics there, which led me to include *Black Athena* in this chapter, and in a subsequent email exchange she explained why she objects to the work. She has, as they say, 'issues' with Bernal's scholarly methods; his argument is, she wrote, 'bolstered with a vast panoply of evidence – very crudely analysed and deployed but bludgeoning the sceptical reader into submission', his translations from key passages of Herodotus are 'economical' and he is, she believes, far too literal in his reading of the way Greek authors 'speculated and mythologised' about the cultural origins of their own civilisation.

But her most serious complaint is that Bernal takes today's concepts of race and racism and uses them to explain a time when people thought about such things in a completely different way. He casts Egypt as part of what we would now call Black Africa, and Professor Beard argues that 'Not only is that, so far as we can see, plain wrong . . . But it is to foist the categories of modern racism onto the ancient world.' The falsification of the past then corrupts modern debate: 'Not far down the line,' she wrote, 'this is conscripted into "live" debates about racism – with black students (especially) trying to fight a valiant (anti-racist) cause with preposterous weapons (such as the "fact" that Cleopatra and Socrates were black).'

Professor Beard acknowledges that the book forced classical scholars to re-examine some of their tired assumptions, but she judges it 'Terrible in its framing of an apparently anti-racist contribution in neo-racist terms'. Like a number of other characters we have met on this journey through a PC World, Bernal is guilty of precisely the kind of intellectual crime of which he accuses others – distorting the past for ideological reasons in a damaging way.

Digging about in Bernal's work with the Professor's strictures in mind, I turned up signs of the dodgy second-hand car salesman approach to evidence that I have encountered in a number of the shadier characters I have met lurking about our PC World. He excuses himself from the duty of looking too hard for facts: 'Proof or certainty is difficult enough to achieve, even in the experimental sciences or documented history,' he writes. 'In the fields with which this work is concerned it is out of the question: all one can hope to find is more or less plausibility . . . Thus debates in these areas should not be judged on the basis of *proof* but merely *competitive plausibility*.' In other words – this at least is how I understand the argument – since you cannot prove anything in a field like this, you are entitled to abandon the search for proof altogether, and focus instead on what is essentially an ideological argument about the way the past is interpreted. I must remember to use the doctrine of 'competitive plausibility' the next time a Cabinet minister accuses me of not knowing my facts during the course of an interview.

This is one of those areas of a PC World which has been much more thoroughly explored in the United States than it has here – and the debate about the teaching of history in America goes right back to those PC skirmishes I described in the first chapter. In 1989 a Task Force on Minorities, Equity and Excellence set up by New York's state government produced a report which concluded that 'African-Americans, Asian-Americans, Puerto Ricans/Latinos and Native Americans have all been victims of an intellectual and educational oppression that has characterized the culture and institutions of the United States and the European American world for centuries.' The impact of that, the report argued, can be seen in a lower than expected level of academic achievement among minorities; 'the systematic bias toward European culture and its derivatives,' it said, had had 'a terribly damaging effect on the psyche of young people of African, Asian, Latin American and Native American descent'. It proposed a reworked curriculum which would give more prominence to the historical contribution non-European cultures had made to the United States so that children from minority communities would have 'higher self-esteem and self-respect, while children from European cultures will have a less arrogant perspective'.

This revisionist approach to teaching history drove thinking in a number of American states during the late

1980s and early 1990s and it provoked – unsurprisingly – a backlash. One of the most eloquent plaints was penned by the late Arthur M. Schlesinger Jr, a Pulitzer Prize-winning historian with impeccable liberal credentials (he worked as a special advisor to President Kennedy and served on the executive council of the *Journal for Negro History*). *The Disuniting of America – Reflections on Multicultural Society* begins with a beautifully written piece of history as poetry, a concise and deeply felt account of the way America became the proverbial melting pot, 'a severing of roots, a liberation from the stifling past, an entry into a new life, an interweaving of separate ethnic strands into a new national design'. But Schlesinger's enthusiasm for the idea of the new beginning that America represents did not mean that he dismissed the power of the past – far from it. In a passage echoed by the Chris McGovern comments I have quoted earlier, he wrote,

history is to the nation rather as memory is to the individual. As an individual deprived of memory becomes disorientated and lost, not knowing where he has been or where he is going, so a nation denied a conception of its past will be disabled in dealing with its present and its future. As the means of defining national identity, history becomes a means of shaping history. The writing of history then turns from a meditation into a weapon.

*The Disuniting of America* was published in 1991, but reading it in the Britain of 2007 – with its buzzing debates about multiculturalism and national identity ringing in my ears – I felt I was reading a prolonged op-ed piece in a contemporary newspaper. When I was halfway through the book the author died – at the age of ninety – which rather added to the queasy sense of time-warp *zeitgeist*. Schlesinger's argument rests on two propositions: that America's new focus on ethnic as opposed to national history threatens to unravel the alchemical knot by which the country has made 'one out of many' – or *e pluribus unum*, as the motto has it – and that history is being distorted to allay the kind of concerns about minority low self-esteem expressed in the report of the New York Task Force I have quoted above. He cites, for example, the history curriculum guide in New York, which told students that there were three foundations of America's constitution: the experience of British colonial rule, the European Enlightenment, and the 'Haudenosaunee political system', a reference to the confederation of Iroquois Native Americans which dominated north-east America before the first Europeans settled here. This system, the guide suggested, was an influence not only on the Founding Fathers of the United States but on the thinking of Locke, Montesquieu, Voltaire and Rousseau. 'How many experts on the American Constitution would endorse this stirring tribute to the "Haudenosaunee political system"? How many have even heard of it?' Schlesinger demands indignantly. 'Whatever influence the Iroquois confederation may have had on the framers of the Constitution was marginal; on European intellectuals it was marginal to the point of invisibility.'

Schlesinger characterises this kind of thing as 'history as therapy', and he points out that it involves suppressing any bits of the past which do not produce the appropriate feel-good reaction in those it is aimed at. 'All major races, cultures, nations,' he writes, 'have committed crimes, atrocities, horrors at one time or another . . . Honest history calls for the unexpurgated record. How much would a full account of African despotism, massacre, and slavery increase the self-esteem of black students? Yet what kind of history do you have if you leave out all the bad things?' Schlesinger's book puts him very firmly in the anti-PC ranks – but that last question is of course precisely the one deployed so powerfully by the PC campaigners who argued that Britain should be more honest about accepting its part in the slave trade.

Almost everyone with whom I have had a social conversation of any length over the past year has offered their own ideas about what I should include in this book, and the vast majority of these dinner party contributions – like Professor Beard's above – have been helpful. But when someone made the rather startling suggestion that I should explore the denazification process which took place in Germany after the Second World War I did feel my heart sinking a little. It was – the argument ran – an illuminating example of a truly successful PC revolution.

All very well, but the story of mid- to late-twentieth-century Germany (Germanies plural, in fact, because the period includes the brief and unlamented existence of the GDR) seemed a rather large chunk of history to bite off in a book like this.

But the thought nagged away at the back of my mind, and I could not resist some research forays into the stacks of the London Library. And the more I read on the subject the more intrigued I became. My dinner companion's case – and you can blame him if you feel it is rather late in the day to be getting stuck into a subject like this – was that denazification was not simply about sacking prominent Nazis or putting on the Nuremberg trials; it also involved a massive campaign to replace the Nazi ideology with a new set of values and a new set of views about the boundaries of acceptable opinion – in other words that the allied victors were essentially trying to change attitudes in very much the same way as campaigners for a PC World are doing today.

That analysis does make some sort of sense when you think of the dilemma that confronted the victorious Allies in 1945. Revenge – for which there was certainly and understandably considerable appetite, particularly among the Russians – was the easy bit. Once you had strung up von Ribbentrop and Co., you still faced the awkward fact that the Nazi Party had had some eight million members while a further four million were members of dependent organisations – so around a fifth of the population were linked with Nazism in a formal way. And there were plenty of voices suggesting that support for Nazism went much wider. Field Marshal Montgomery is reported to have said, before he left Germany in May 1946, that three-quarters of the population were 'hard-bitten Nazis'.

The implications of accepting that Nazism was simply too well entrenched in Germany to be eradicated would have been grim indeed; it would have meant accepting the existence of a dangerous and destabilising force at the heart of Europe in perpetuity. So there had to be some kind of redemptive possibility – a hope that all those minds could be changed to think in a more 'politically correct' way. That was presumably what Churchill had in mind when he told the House of Commons, towards the end of May 1944, that 'We will fight on together until Nazism is extirpated . . .'; the phrase implied that Nazism was something that could be removed from Germany, almost like a cancer. Germany needed a new post-Hitler identity.

But how could this be done? Nothing quite like it had ever been tried before. In view of the scale and unprecedented nature of the task it is perhaps unsurprising that denazification produced a deal of chaos and some (unintentionally) hilarious consequences. There was considerable discussion of the 'German national character' and the question of whether it was naturally inclined to militarism and authoritarianism. Michael Balfour, a historian who served as director of information services in the British zone in 1946 and later wrote a magisterial scholarly account of *Four-Power Control in Germany and Austria 1945–1946*, gets into some very un-PC hot water when he strays beyond the boundaries of his academic discipline and speculates about a link between Nazism and a latent homosexual tendency in German culture.

The society held up for admiration by many German writers has been essentially a masculine one, exalting manliness and hardness to an extent that suggested a subconscious compensating inclination to the opposite. Exhibitions of tenderness and of interests associated with feminine values were deplored . . . By men of this outlook, weakness was not only despised but charity and tolerance were confused with it. By contrast, however, Germans lapsed all too easily into excessive sentimentality, to which the very language lends itself. In the light of modern psychological knowledge it is impossible to avoid seeing a connexion between this ambivalence and the phenomena of homosexuality.

So there you are, then – all those stormtroopers were just gay guys struggling to stay in the closet!

Also the subject of much lampooning was the so-called *Fragenbogen*, the twelve-page form containing nearly 150 questions which was designed to establish whether or not people had Nazi sympathies. Even amid the misery of total defeat, some Germans were able to find a glimmer of humour in the fact that they were asked whether the

Allied bombing of their cities had affected their health, work or sleep! And the document illustrates the pitfalls of the PC-ist habit of defining people on the basis of checklists. Those completing it were asked whether they had any scars – even though the duelling fraternities with which these were associated had been banned by Hitler – and whether they had family connections to the Junker nobility; this last requirement was especially odd in the light of the fact that most of those involved in the July 1944 attempt on Hitler's life were aristocrats. One woman with a smart name (including the aristocratic particle 'von') remarked, 'In the old days it was having a Jewish grandmother that caused problems, now it is having a noble one.'

Each of the occupying powers went about the process of denazification in a slightly different way – bear with me while I spend a little time exploring them, because I think they tell us something about the temptations and obstacles involved in trying to build a PC World. The Americans pursued the business with vengeful rigour and thoroughness. The basis of the American approach was an extraordinary document known as 'JCS 1067' – JCS being the initials of the Joint Chiefs of Staff in Washington. The punitive spirit behind it is clear from the instruction to America's senior officers to keep the Germans living on the breadline; they were told to 'estimate requirements of supplies necessary to prevent starvation or widespread disease or such civil unrest as would endanger the occupying forces' but at the same time to ensure that German 'consumption be held to a minimum'. Any surplus was to be used by the occupying forces, and 'basic living standards in Germany' must not be allowed to rise above those of neighbouring countries.

The document's definition of those who should be drawn within the net of the trawl for Nazis is astonishingly broad – and it is impossible to read it without thinking about the disastrous American policy of de-Bathification in Iraq after the toppling of Saddam Hussein. Paragraph 6 of JCS 1067 lays out the following instructions:

All members of the Nazi Party who have been more than nominal participants in its activities, all active supporters of Nazism or militarism and all other persons hostile to Allied purposes will be removed and excluded from positions of importance in quasi-public and private enterprises such as (1) civic, economic and labour organisations, (2) corporations and other organisations in which the German government or subdivisions have a major financial interest, (3) industry, commerce, agriculture, and finance, (4), education, (5), the press, publishing houses and other agencies disseminating news and propaganda. Persons are to be treated as more than nominal participants in party activities and as active supporters of Nazism or militarism when they have (1) held office or otherwise been active at any level from local to national in the party or its subordinate organisations, or in organisations which further militaristic doctrines, (2) authorised or participated formally in Nazi war crimes, racial persecutions or discriminations, (3) been avowed believers in Nazism or racial and militaristic creeds, or (4) voluntarily given substantial moral or material support or political assistance of any kind to the Nazi Party or Nazi officials and leaders. No such persons shall be retained in any of the categories of employment listed above because of administrative necessity, or convenience or expediency.

The Americans tried an astonishing 169,282 cases during the denazification process – to put that into perspective, the figures for the French and Russian zones were around 17,000 and 18,000 respectively, for the British only a little over 2,000. The American assault on Nazism was cultural too; when the United States army took the Wagnerian shrine of Bayreuth (reducing a third of it to rubble in the process) they immediately banned the playing of Wagner's music. General Lucius Clay, the man running the zone under the control of the United States forces, was an enthusiastic banner of books thought to have a militaristic or Nazi flavour – a strategy which was awkwardly reminiscent of the Nazi habit of burning books.

Come the first serious signs of the Cold War and American policy went into reverse; in 1949 the Americans began to release those convicted of Nazi crimes in large numbers. One wonders if anyone thought of discussing this instructive episode in America's history with Paul Bremer, George Bush's viceroy in Baghdad and the man responsible for the de-Bathification process which is now acknowledged to have done so much damage in Iraq.

The Russian policy for dealing with denazification failed for different reasons. The Soviet authorities used the history of the Nazi period to bolster the ideological under-pinning for Communism in their newly created client state of East Germany (or the German Democratic Republic, to give it its formal title). The strategy was to represent the Nazi phenomenon as something foisted on ordinary Germans by class enemies. The Jewish writer Amos Elon visited East Germany in the mid 1960s and listened in during a history session as a young student gave this account of German history in the 1930s and 1940s: 'The fascistic terror regime in Germany started in January 1933. Imperialistic elements of capitalism joined with *Wehrmacht* officers to exterminate the German communist party. They murdered many workers and Jews in concentration camps. The people suffered terribly. Several attempts were made to shoot Hitler.' In Leipzig a dissident Social Democrat tells him, 'here the subject is treated as a Congo massacre, planned and executed by some imperialist capitalists . . . This massacre has nothing to do with us personally – with the history of our country, our fathers, uncles, cousins, mothers, aunts and nieces. Not flesh and blood was responsible for Auschwitz, we are told, but an anonymous system which still exists in Bonn.'

Britain's denazification efforts were much criticised in

the British press and Parliament for being ramshackle
and lacking clarity. And many Germans were offended
by the superior way in which British officers treated them,
complaining that they were being reduced to 'a *kolonial-
volk* – a colonial people like the Indians' (let us not
even begin to try to unravel the layers of non-PC senti-
ment in that statement). But there was one decision taken
by the British authorities which attracts almost universal
praise in histories of this period, and it played very much
to the British reputation for inspired eccentricity: the
reorganisation of education in the British zone of occu-
pied Germany was placed in the hands of the man who
was shortly to become the headmaster of Eton.

Robert Birley was a historian, and he brought a historian's perspective to the task in hand. He understood that
before Germany could enjoy a new identity the country
needed a new understanding of its past, and in that sense
he was probably more responsible than anyone else for
the idea that denazification needed to be a mind-changing
exercise in 'Political Correctness'. 'We occupy a country
without a government,' he later wrote, 'and from the
outset our occupying forces had not only to prevent the
revival of military danger, they had to rebuild a community.' Giles MacDonogh, in his recently published history
of post-war Germany, records that Birley had been
shocked by what he saw in a chapel in the Czech city of
Brno: 'The SS had turned it over to paganism. The altar
had been mounted by a giant swastika containing a copy

of *Mein Kampf* and an immense eagle decorated the wall in place of the reredos. The British needed to change the minds and outlook of the people who did such a thing . . .' Birley's methods sound charmingly quaint: German academics were sent to Wilton Park, a former PoW camp in Buckinghamshire, for re-education. But this form of 're-education' had none of the sinister connotations the word acquired in late twentieth-century totalitarian regimes. The courses were under the direction of a German academic who had gone to Oxford in the 1930s and stayed on during the war, and they were run very much along Oxbridge lines; there were one-to-one tutorials, energetic and free-ranging discussion was encouraged, and the students were served their meals as if eating at High Table.

'*Au fond*,' MacDonogh writes, 'the British believed more in re-education than in denazification.' The instinct was the right one, and in time it would bear fruit in the success of the concept of *Vergangenheitsbewaltigung*, one of those gloriously clumsy but useful German compounds which means, very roughly, 'coming to terms with the past'. But in the reading I have done for this book I have been struck by how long it took the Germans to do that. One of Birley's assistants, Raymond Ebsworth, wrote of the difficulty of dealing with Nazi history in school text-books: 'What was done in many Lander,' he recorded, 'was simply to ignore the Nazi period altogether, or to dismiss it in a few paragraphs. It was some years before

it was realised that this simply would not do ...' Even
fifteen years after the end of the war (Ebsworth's book
was published in 1960), the author was uncertain about
'whether this belated attempt to show young people the
evils of Nazism will be successful'.

Amos Elon's *Journey through a Haunted Land*, written
a few years later, offers some graphic illustrations of the
non-PC habit of mind that persisted into the 1960s. The
1963 edition of Kupper's *Dictionary of Everyday Usage*
contained a set of definitions which takes us right back
to George Orwell in Chapter 2:

*Nazi* (noun)
1 Ridiculous, dumb man; word of abuse abbreviated from the
  first name Ingatz, Ignatius
2 Austrian soldier, Austrian
3 National Socialist
4 'That's enough to make the biggest Nazi leave the party'; an
  expression of ill humour, despair

Elon also quotes a 1961 textbook which records that 'Jews
from all over Europe were cruelly murdered in special
extermination camps erected by Hitler. However, the
German people were informed of the full extent of these
atrocities only after the war.' Another (published in 1960)
calls the extermination camps 'intensified measures
against the Jews', and still another (of the same vintage),
with a flourish of bathos which would be wonderful were

not the subject so serious, says of the camps: 'Hundreds of thousands of Jews lost their lives here, or at least their health.'

One of the best accounts of Germany's long journey back to a healthy relationship with its past is *The German Trauma – Experiences and Reflections 1938–2000*, written by another great student of guilt and memory, Gitta Sereny. The book is a collection of essays, and its value lies both in the span of time it covers – which gives a sense of the pace of change in Germany – and in the reporting skills of the author. Sereny's writing is full of judgement and colour, but what really makes it powerful is her determination to collect and record the facts – she does pre-eminently well what all of us in the trade of journalism should be trying to do.

Sereny argues that in the end it was the Germans themselves – or at least certain sections of German society – who grappled with the past in a way that made a difference. While she allows that it was years before the history of the Third Reich was properly taught in schools, she writes that

the world has never recognised the extent to which by contrast writers, film-makers and the media concentrated on the subject from very early on – from the early 1950s – soon producing a veritable stream of books, commentaries and debates of considerable quality, all focusing on the moral degeneracy of the Nazis . . . And I believe that it was this intense preoccupation with their country's past . . . even more than the Marshall Plan and the resultant *Wirtschaftswunder*, that has been the source of Germany's remarkable moral recovery.

Among the most gripping of these essays is Sereny's account of a visit to West Germany in the late 1960s, when the country, after regaining its sovereignty, was carrying out its own trials for crimes committed during the Nazi era. The process involved tens of thousands of investigations and continued for more than two decades. Many of the cases were meticulously and regularly reported in the press, and some lasted for months or even years. Talking to young people in schools and clubs, Sereny found a deep – and understandable – resistance to the way they were being forced to confront what their parents' generation had done. She sat in on some of the trials herself:

Perhaps the greatest shock comes because the proceedings, on the face of it, are so terribly ordinary.

The seats for the public are often filled with boys and girls – school classes brought by young teachers. The children munch sweets and chocolates. They chat and giggle.

Ten feet away, on three benches, sit the accused. Well dressed, ruddy faced, they too talk and laugh together. Defence counsel in black robes walk up and down the tiers, stop here and there, say a word, a smile, touch a shoulder.

. . .

The first defendant is called to the stand – a table and a chair in the centre of the room, a microphone on the table. He walks the few steps to this seat very quickly. He is a man of fifty-two, married, three children. Profession: grocer. He sits with his back to us.

The judge: 'Herr R., let me just read to you what this part of the accusation says, and then we'll see what you have to say about it.' He reads, without expression: 'Johann R. is accused, as SS chief of guards of the forced labour camp T in June 1943, in the course of the liquidation of the city's ghetto, to have caught about sixty children under ten years of age who had tried to hide . . . to have stood them up alongside a pit, to have killed them individually through repeated blows on their heads with a hammer, whereupon the bodies fell into the pit, while the parents were forced to watch.'

The children behind me had stopped their fidgeting. Some were sitting very still; others had craned forward to hear better; a few had blushed, gone pale. The young teacher had been sitting, her chin supported by her hand. For a moment she leaned back and covered her eyes.

Judge: 'Well now, Herr R., you've heard the accusation. What do you have to say?'

R. (portentous and fluent): 'I want to do everything to help the court, of course, but it was so long ago.'

Judge: 'One could hardly forget such a scene – unless of course it happened so often . . .' He left the sentence hanging in the air.

Those children stopping their fidgeting and craning forward to hear better represent as vivid an image of the power of history in action as one could wish for. Truth is what made a difference in Germany – not the book- and music-banning of the Americans or the Soviet attempt to write personal guilt out of East Germany's past. It may have taken at least a quarter of a century and it may have been an extremely painful process, but in the end the country did come to terms with its past – by looking with clear eyes at what really happened. One of the lawyers involved in prosecuting those responsible for the atrocities of the Nazi era told Gitta Sereny,

The day will never come when we say 'it is done now, it's finished'. There is no end to it except a biological one, when at last they will all be dead. And *then* it will only be finished if, in the meantime, we have succeeded in teaching those who come after us. The only guarantee of it never happening again is knowledge.

He was right – an enterprise of this kind can never really finish. Forty years later, as I was writing this chapter, a comic-book story about the Holocaust – drawn, somewhat ironically, in the style of Tintin – was introduced to schools in Berlin amid concern that the latest generation of Germans know too little about their country's past. At the same time a new dictionary was published to remind Germans of the historical baggage attached to some well-known words and

245

phrases; it points out, for example, that *endlosung* or 'final solution' ought not to be used to mean the answer to a difficult problem – an example of the PC use of language that none of us, surely, would quibble with. And at about the same time a young German television presenter lost her job for using the phrase *Arbeit Macht Frei* – 'Work Makes Free', the slogan above the gates at Auschwitz – in a jokey way on the air.

Is Germany's story really relevant to an understanding of today's PC World? I think it is.

At the beginning of this exploration of our PC World I described it as a navigation of the difficult waters between a shockingly un-PC member of the royal family and a military man who was simply feckless in his choice of words, and I am sure many of you have been irritated by the way I have zigzagged across the currents, tacking back and forth in my opinions without warning. By way of apology I offer this thought: like the Siren voices which nearly distracted Odysseus from a true course as he sailed home from Troy, PC-ers have a genuinely appealing song to sing. PC may not be a properly formulated political programme, but it is, in the best sense of the term, a liberal dream, an expression of the conviction that the world can be made a better place. At its heart lie very basic and simple aspirations – that we should not be insulted because of the colour of our skin, for example, or suffer discrimination because we are disabled. PC is fired by a faith in fairness – and of course that is appealing.

Looking back through what I have written, I am struck by the number of times I have wanted to acknowledge that the PC agenda is driven by the best of intentions.

But the rocky realities of Scylla and Charybdis were every bit as much of a threat to Odysseus's journey as the seductive voices of the Sirens. Again and again I have found that the dreamy aspirations of Political Correctness have tempted its enthusiasts to distort reality and lie about the world as it really is. The really good writers I have used to guide me on my journey – thinkers like John Stuart Mill and George Orwell, reporters like Gitta Sereny – understand the dangers of that, and the German example suggests it is perhaps most important of all when it comes to the way we tell the story of our past. In a very small way I know from my own experience how important it is to use experience and reality as checks on opinion and comment in the way we represent the world; every so often I escape from the *Today* programme studio to report at first hand from somewhere like Iraq or Afghanistan, and it is like a cold, head-clearing shower after all those fuggy mornings of spin in the studio.

Thirty years in public broadcasting have left me extremely cautious about passing judgement – you get so used to picking apart the opinions of others that you eventually lose the capacity to have any of your own – but at the end of my own odyssey through a PC World I would like to issue a few anathemas: to those who would cut words from their meanings; to those who think history

247

can be rewritten for the sake of ideological convenience; to philosophers – like the structuralists – who think that their own cleverness matters more than objective truth; to peddlers of theories of 'comparative plausibility' and the like; to politicians who think they can force us to imagine their dreams into being, whether we like them or not, and even when they fly in the face of the world as it really is; to those who ignore harm in the name of tolerance, like the police officers who wink at honour killing; to those who think beauty matters less than social manipulation, like the modern art critics who make such a mockery of the subject they study; and most of all to those who would place limits on the way we write, speak and think in the name of their social and political goals. To all of the above I say – in a very caring way, of course – 'You threaten the very values you claim to promote. Go boil your heads.'

# Select bibliography

For an insight into what became known as the 'culture wars' in the United States, I would recommend the following books:

Aufderheide, Patricia (ed.), *Beyond PC: Towards a Politics of Understanding* (Graywold Press, St Paul, Minnesota, 1992).

Berman, Paul (ed.), *Debating PC: The Controversy over Political Correctness on College Campuses* (Dell, New York, 1993).

Bloom, Allan, *The Closing of the American Mind* (Simon and Schuster, New York, 1987).

Buchanan, Patrick J., *The Death of the West* (Thomas Dunne Books, New York, 2002).

Cronin, Blaise, *Jeremiad Jottings* (The Scarecrow Press, Lanham, Maryland, and Oxford, 2004).

Fish, Stanley, *Professional Correctness* (Clarendon Press, Oxford, 1995).

Hughes, Robert, *Culture of Complaint: The Fraying of America* (HarperCollins, London, 1993).

Ravitch, Diane, *The Language Police: How Pressure Groups Restrict What Students Learn* (Vintage Books, New York, 2004).

Roiphe, Katie, *The Morning After: Sex, Fear and Feminism* (Hamish Hamilton, London, 1994).

The collection of essays edited by Sarah Dunant (*War of Words: The Political Correctness Debate*, Virago, London, 1994) is a good place to start exploring PC in Britain. There are any number of pamphlets published by Civitas (*The Retreat of Reason* by Anthony Browne, *The Corruption of the Curriculum* edited by Robert Whelan and *We're (Nearly) All Victims Now!*, by David Green) and the Institute for Public Policy Research (*The Power of Belonging* by Ben Rogers and Rick Muir) which give a flavour of the current state of the British debate on both sides. *Littlejohn's Britain* (by Richard Littlejohn; Hutchinson, London, 2007) carries an endorsement from Jeremy Clarkson describing it as 'Savage, hilarious, a fantastic read', and James Delingpole's book, *How to be Right: The Indispensable Guide to Making Lefty Liberals*

*History*, was published by Headline in 2007. Aidan Rankin's *The Politics of the Forked Tongue: Authoritarian Liberalism* (New European Publications, London, 2002) is terse and to the point.

For a discussion of PC language I recommend Deborah Cameron's *Verbal Hygiene* (Routledge, London, 1995). On the subject of art, Roger Kimball's *The Rape of the Masters: How Political Correctness Sabotages Art* (Encounter Books, San Francisco, 2004) offers great pleasure. Arthur M. Schlesinger Jr's *The Disuniting of America* (Whittle Direct Books, Knoxville, Tennessee, 1991) is best on history.

I used Maurice Ashley's *Oliver Cromwell and the Puritan Revolution* (English Universities Press, London, 1958) for the story of seventeenth-century PC-ness. Those interested in the story of denazification in post-war Germany should try the following:

Balfour, Michael, and Mair, John, *Four-Power Control in Germany and Austria, 1945–1946* (Oxford University Press, Oxford, 1956).

Ebsworth, Raymond, *Restoring Democracy* (Stevens and Sons, London, 1960).

Elon, Amos, *Journey through a Haunted Land* (André Deutsch, London, 1963).

Horne, Alistair, *Back into Power* (Max Parrish, London, 1955).

Sereny, Gitta, *The German Trauma: Experience and Reflections 1938–2000* (Allen Lane, London, 2000).

# Index

# Index

# Index

# Index

# Index

Williams, Archbishop of Canterbury
  Rowan 10–11, 162–3
Winterval myth 200
Wookey, Charles 149–50

**Y**

Year of Revolutions (1989) 32
York Mystery Plays, fourteenth
  century 6–7, 8, 10
Younge, Gary 220–1
Youth in the 1980s 31–2